NOTES OF A NATIVE SON

JAMES BALDWIN

With a New Introduction by
Edward P. Jones

Beacon Press, Boston

BEACON PRESS
25 Beacon Street
Boston, MA 02108-2892
www.beacon.org

Beacon Press books are published under
the auspices of the Unitarian Universalist
Association of Congregations.

First edition published by Beacon Press in 1955
First Beacon paperback published in 1957

Text design and composition by Kim Arney

Library of Congress Cataloging-in-Publication Data

Baldwin, James, 1924–1987.
    Notes of a native son / James Baldwin ; with a new
introduction by Edward P. Jones. — Revised ed.
        p. cm.
    Includes bibliographical references.
    ISBN 978-0-8070-0611-5 (cloth : acid-free paper)
    ISBN 978-0-8070-0623-8 (pbk. : acid-free paper)
1. African Americans—Civil rights. 2. African
Americans—Social conditions—To 1964. 3. United
States—Race relations. 4. Baldwin, James, 1924–1987.
I. Jones, Edward P. II. Title.
    E185.61.B2 2012
    305.8'96073—dc23   2012021246

FOR
PAULA MARIA
AND
GEBRIL

Contents

Introduction by Edward P. Jones   *vii*

Acknowledgments   *xv*

Preface to the 1984 Edition   *xvii*

Autobiographical Notes   3

PART ONE

Everybody's Protest Novel   13

Many Thousands Gone   25

Carmen Jones: The Dark Is Light Enough   47

PART TWO

The Harlem Ghetto   59

Journey to Atlanta   75

Notes of a Native Son   87

PART THREE

Encounter on the Seine: Black Meets Brown   119

A Question of Identity   127

Equal in Paris   141

Stranger in the Village   163

Introduction

I did not know James Baldwin the essayist before my first year of college. I knew only the James Baldwin of novels and short stories and plays, a trusted man who gave me, with his Harlem and his Harlem people, the kind of world I knew so well from growing up in my Washington, D.C. They were all one family, the people in Harlem and the people in Washington, Baldwin told me in that way of all grand and eloquent writers who speak the eternal and universal by telling us, word by hard-won word, of the minutiae of the everyday: The church ladies who put heart and soul into every church service as if to let their god know how worthy they are to step through the door into his heaven. The dust of poor folks' apartments that forever hangs in the air as though to remind the people of their station in life. The streets of a city where the buildings Negroes live in never stand straight up but lean in mourning every which way.

So I knew this Baldwin and, in that strange way of members of the same family, he knew me. When I went off to college in late August 1968, I took few books, anticipating the adequacy of the library that awaited me at Holy Cross College. I packed only two books of nonfiction, both bought in a used bookstore not long after I was accepted to college. Both had never been read. The first was a ponderous 1950s

tome on writing logical and well-reasoned essays. I was never
to read it in my time at Holy Cross, perhaps because it was
so inaccessible. (Seeing it on my dormitory room's bookshelf,
Clarence Thomas, a month before his graduation from Holy
Cross in 1971, purchased the book from me for $5; I do not
recall what I paid for it.) And the second was *Notes of a Native Son*. I was going off to a new life, a life of the mind and
education among white people, and I felt that since Baldwin's fiction had taught me so much about black people, his
essays might have a similar effect given where I was going.

I entered Holy Cross as a mathematics major, primarily
because I had done well in math in high school. I was extremely shy then, and I had never had my vision tested and
did not know enough about anything to realize that my frequent inability to see the blackboard could be solved with
eyeglasses. I sat in the back of the freshman calculus class
run by a standoffish professor who spent most of the period
with his back to his students as he wrote on the blackboard,
and with all of that, I fell further and further behind as the
semester progressed.

I will go into English, I told myself in December, knowing
how much I loved to read and knowing that a calculus D was
coming and so there would be no life in mathematics. Before
leaving for Christmas vacation, I picked up *Notes of a Native
Son* for the first time, perhaps understanding that now my
life would be increasingly one of essay writing. The first thing
James Baldwin tells me in "Autobiographical Notes" is, "I
was born in Harlem. . . ." A simple, unadorned statement, as
if in saying it plainly the reader would have a better sense of
the importance of that fact. It was Harlem, but because I was
so familiar with the Baldwin of fiction, the Baldwin whose

black people could be Washingtonians, he could only have begun to connect in a better way if he had said, "I was born in Washington, D.C. . . ."

A good bit of that introductory essay deals with being a writer, something that would not have much meaning for me for many years: the necessity of delving into oneself to be able to tell the truth about the world one writes about; the difficulties of being a Negro writer when "the Negro problem" is so widely written about; the desire, at the end of the day, to be "a good writer."

But within that short essay is a thirty-one-year-old, somewhat worldly man (I did not get my first passport until I was fifty-four) who is still grappling with having been born into a small and often less than caring world, which was, for good or bad, a part of a larger world that generally rejected him and his small world. I was a Holy Cross student—often happy to be a student at "the Cross"—but I knew every time I stepped out of my room in Beaven dormitory that no part of that place in Worcester, Massachusetts, had been made with me in mind. I felt that but did not yet have very many words for it. Baldwin gave them to me. This is Baldwin, with his "special attitude," talking of Shakespeare and the cathedral at Chartres and Rembrandt and the Empire State Building and Bach: "These were not really my creations, they did not contain my history; I might search in them in vain forever for any reflection of myself. I was an interloper; this was not my heritage."

And so he continued throughout the rest of *Notes*, a gloriously keen and sensitive mind, something I did not completely appreciate at the time, something I'm sure he would smile about now. I confess that I could not then grasp some of his more complex thoughts, perhaps because I was merely too young and the world had yet to take such a harsh hold on me. And other thoughts of his I just dismissed, no doubt because I was, again, too young and because I was developing a militant streak that scoffed at notions not in line with my own developing ones. That militancy came naturally with the murder of Martin Luther King Jr. and the Vietnam War and with the new awareness that I was black in a white world. The militant me asked, for example, why would Baldwin write at times as if he were not black but some observer, a guilty one, true, but still an observer. "Our dehumanization of the Negro then," he says to me in "Many Thousands Gone," "is indivisible from dehumanization of ourselves: the loss of our own identity is the price we pay for our annulment of his." And later: "We (Americans in general, that) like to point to Negroes and to most of their activities with a kind of tolerant scorn. . . ."

But with my focus on the constant use of words like "we" and "our," it was easy for eighteen-year-old me in those last days of December 1968 to lose sight of so much of the truth and pain of that and other statements in "Thousands." People, I have learned, have a way of taking root in one's still-developing mind without our knowing it, especially people, like Baldwin, who live in the world of words. How else, then, to explain my every effort to tell in a novel as best I could the stories of slave masters, black and white, and how slavery crushed their souls every morning they got up from their beds and thanked their god for their dominion over others. If I knew the importance of telling that, it was because Baldwin and his kind had planted the idea long ago. (I give him so much credit because he was in the minority of all the black writers I was reading who understood the importance of giving white people their due as full-fledged human beings. Even before I knew I would get into this writing thing, Baldwin told me this: You do not have to fully humanize your black characters by dehumanizing the white ones.)

Traveling with Baldwin through *Notes'* "The Harlem Ghetto," "Journey to Atlanta," and "Notes of a Native Son," I was given a grander portrait of the man I had known only through fiction. His fiction certainly had an unprecedented and absolute life of its own, and I might have tried to imagine the man I was dealing with, but those essays afforded me something beyond the postage stamp–sized pictures of him and the few sentences of biography that came with my paperback editions of, say, *Go Tell It on the Mountain* or *Another Country*. He would have been Baldwin had I never read those essays, but he would not have been real enough to deign to share a moment or two with me. The fiction offered a person of enormous humanity. The essays offered a man, a neighbor, or, yes, an older brother.

I had gone through the Washington, D.C., riots after King's assassination, an explosion that took place some twenty-five years after the Harlem riots Baldwin describes in "Notes." Different city, different actors, but the same script as that used in the nationwide riots of the 1910s, also a conflagration that included Washington. I was mainly on the periphery of matters that April 1968. (My poor mother had enough to worry about; the last thing I wanted was to add another thousand pounds to her burden and have her see her college-bound child in jail.) And with a summer job and college looming, I had not had time to assess my feelings or consider those of my classmates or neighbors. The wonderful thing about writers like Baldwin is the way we read them and come across passages that are so arresting we become breathless and have to raise our eyes from the page to keep from being spirited away. During those few days in April, I had been out and about enough in my city to sense something new and different about all the shouting and window-breaking and looting people, something ancient and deep. This is Baldwin explaining to me in words written twelve years after the Harlem riots and thirteen years before the Washington riots: "[S]omething heavy in their stance seemed to indicate that they had all, incredibly, seen a common vision, and on each face there seemed to be the same strange, bitter shadow."

Time after time, he keeps doing this so that it becomes not enough for the reader to just raise the eyes to find breath again. In "Equal in Paris," there is the sad tale of Baldwin being jailed for days during Christmastime in 1949 after being given a used hotel sheet he did not know had been stolen. Yes. Days. Used sheet. One does not understand the full meaning of "Kafkaesque" until this tale has been absorbed. Baldwin does not say it outright, but what becomes clear with his journey through a perversely blind justice system is that France, for "all the wretched," had not moved very far from what the people were enduring before the French Revolution.

It is all so utterly absurd (and this absurdity is another layer of oppression) that it truly becomes humorous. And with that as well is Baldwin's realization that the people who run such a system are first cousins of those who run things in "my native land." He cannot escape them, even in a place called Paris, and he is better for knowing this. "In some deep, black, stony,

and liberating way, my life, in my own eyes, began during
that first year in Paris. . . ."

And so he continues on, page after page, offering light and
understanding and a ruthless insistence not so much that he
is correct with his vision of matters, but that to ignore his side
of things is to see only a partial picture that will not lead to
lasting solutions. I can see this best now that I have reread
Notes for this essay and now that life has done things to me.
Which is why his book is to be treasured. In small ways, in
large ways.

Of the *Amsterdam Star-News*, he notes in "The Harlem
Ghetto" that it "is Republican [no doubt the legacy of Abraham Lincoln freeing the slaves with the belief that it would
shorten the Civil War], a political affiliation that has led it into
some strange doubletalk. . . ." I had to chuckle. He was writing of possibly gentler, kinder Republicans, who were, in a
matter of years, to grow into even more vicious and uncar-
ing political animals. I do not know if Baldwin witnessed any
of what happened when black conservatives came out of the
woodwork during Ronald Reagan's presidency. A collection of
blacks who to this day have to defend all the white racists in
the various spokes of the Republican Party wheel. Doubletalk.

And the entire essay "Journey to Atlanta" is a grand cau-
tionary story about black politicians and white radicals and
liberals, who with their own doubletalk seek to mask a pater-
nalism that sees black people as no more than children. As
I read his words again, I kept thinking of all the white liberals around Washington, D.C., who wrote racist comments in
2010 to area newspapers and blogs after the black mayor (a

rather reviled figure among many black folks) was defeated by another black candidate, complaining that "nigger" voters simply did not know what was good for them. Baldwin—with his tale of his teenage brother David going South—offered his warning in 1948.

One of the wonders of coming back to *Notes* after such a long time is how "current" Baldwin is. That might sound like a cliché, but in so many instances in our lives we learn that some clichés are built on things solid and familiar and timeless. "Journey to Atlanta" is but one of a hundred examples in *Notes*. What also comes across, again, is how optimistic James Baldwin was about himself, his world, black people. Even when he describes the awfulness of being black in America, he presents us with an optimism that is sometimes like subtle background music, and sometimes like an insistent drumbeat. But through it all, with each word—perhaps as evidence of a man certain of his message—he never shouts.

—Edward P. Jones
June 29–July 5, 2012
Washington, D.C.

Acknowledgments

The author is grateful to the following publications for permission to reprint material that first appeared in their pages: *Commentary* for "Carmen Jones" (which appeared in the January 1955 issue as "Life Straight in De Eye"), "The Harlem Ghetto" (February 1948), and "Equal in Paris" (March 1955); *Harper's Magazine* for "Notes of a Native Son" (November 1955) and "Stranger in the Village" (October 1953); *The New Leader* for "Journey to Atlanta" (October 9, 1948); *Partisan Review* for "Everybody's Protest Novel" (June 1949), "Many Thousands Gone" (November-December 1951), and "A Question of Identity" (July-August 1954); and *The Reporter* for "Encounter on the Seine" (which appeared in the issue of June 6, 1950, as "The Negro in Paris").

Preface to the 1984 Edition

James Baldwin

It was Sol Stein, high school buddy, editor, novelist, play-wright, who first suggested this book. My reaction was not enthusiastic: as I remember, I told him that I was too young to publish my memoirs.

I had never thought of these essays as a possible book. Once they were behind me, I don't, in fact, think that I thought of them at all. Sol's suggestion had the startling and unkind effect of causing me to realize that time had passed. It was as though he had dashed cold water in my face.

Sol persisted, however, and so did the dangers and rigors of my situation. I had returned from Paris, in 1954, out of motives not at all clear to me. I had promised a Swiss friend a visit to the land of my birth, but that, I think, has to be rec-ognized as a pretext: it fails to have the weight of a motive. I find no objective reason for my return to America at that time—I am not sure that I can find the subjective one, either.

Yet, here I was, at the top of 1954, several months shy of thirty, scared to death, but happy to be with my family and my friends. It was my second return since my departure, in 1948.

I had returned in 1952, with my first novel, stayed long enough to show it to my family, and to sell it, and, then, I hauled on out of here. In 1954, I came back with *The Amen Corner*, and I was working on *Giovanni's Room*—which had broken off from what was to become *Another Country*.

Actually, '54–'55, in spite of frightening moments, and not only in retrospect, was a great year. I had, after all, survived something—the proof was that I was working. I was at the Writer's Colony, Yaddo, in Saratoga Springs, when my buddy, Marlon Brando, won the Oscar, and I watched Bette Davis present it to him, and kiss him, on TV. The late Owen Dodson called me there, from Washington, D.C., to say that he was directing, at Howard University, a student production of my play. I went to Washington, where I met the late, great E. Franklin Frazier and the great Sterling Brown. Howard was the first college campus I had ever seen, and, without these men, I do not know what would have become of my morale. The play, thank God, was a tremendous seven-or ten-day wonder, playing to standing room only on the last night, in spite of a reluctant, not yet Black faculty ("This play will set back the Speech Department by thirty years!"), a bewildered *Variety* ("What do you think Negroes in the North will think of this play?"), and the fact that it was not to be seen again for nearly ten years. And I had fallen in love. I was happy—the world had never before been so beautiful a place.

There was only one small hitch. I—we—didn't have a dime, no pot, nor no window.

Sol Stein returned to the attack. We had agreed on nine essays, he wanted a tenth, and I wrote the title essay between Owen's house and the Dunbar Hotel. Returned to New York, where I finished *Giovanni's Room*. Publisher's Row, that hotbed of perception, looked on the book with horror and loathing, refused to touch it, saying that I was a young *Negro* writer, who, if he published this book, would alienate his audience and ruin his career. They would not, in short, publish it, as a favor to me. I conveyed my gratitude, perhaps a shade too sharply, borrowed money from a friend, and myself and my lover took the boat to France.

I had never thought of myself as an essayist: the idea had never entered my mind. Even—or, perhaps, especially now—I find it hard to re-create the journey.

It has something to do, certainly, with what I was trying to discover and, also, trying to avoid. If I was trying to discover myself—on the whole, when examined, a somewhat dubious notion, since I was also trying to avoid myself—there was, certainly, between that self and me, the accumulated rock of ages. This rock scarred the hand, and all tools broke against it. Yet, there was a *me,* somewhere: I could feel it, stirring within and against captivity. The hope of salvation—identity—depended on whether or not one would be able to decipher and describe the rock.

One song cries, *"lead me to the rock that is higher than I,"* and another cries, *"hide me in the rock!"* and yet another proclaims, *"I got a home in that rock."* Or, *"I ran to the rock to hide my face: the rock cried out, no hiding place!"*

The accumulated rock of ages deciphered itself as a part of my inheritance—a part, mind you, not the totality—but, in order to claim my birthright, of which my inheritance was but a shadow, it was necessary to challenge and claim the rock. Otherwise, the rock claimed me.

Or, to put it another way, my inheritance was particular, specifically limited and limiting: my birthright was vast, connecting me to all that lives, and to everyone, forever. But one cannot claim the birthright without accepting the inheritance.

Therefore, when I began, seriously, to write—when I knew I was committed, that this would be my life—I had to try to describe that particular condition which was—is—the living proof of my inheritance. And, at the same time, with that very same description, I had to claim my birthright. I am what time, circumstance, history, have made of me, certainly, but I am, also, much more than that. So are we all.

The conundrum of color is the inheritance of every American, be he/she legally or actually Black or White. It is a fearful inheritance, for which untold multitudes, long ago, sold their birthright. Multitudes are doing so, until today. This horror has so welded past and present that it is virtually impossible and certainly meaningless to speak of it as occurring, as it were, in time. It can be, and it has been, suicidal to attempt to speak of this to a multitude, which, assuming it knows that time exists, believes that time can be outwitted.

Something like this, anyway, has something to do with my beginnings. I was trying to locate myself within a specific inheritance and to use that inheritance, precisely, to claim the birthright from which that inheritance had so brutally and specifically excluded me.

It is not pleasant to be forced to recognize, more than thirty years later, that neither this dynamic nor this necessity have changed. There have been superficial changes, with results at best ambiguous and, at worst, disastrous. Morally, there has been no change at all and a moral change is the only real one. "*Plus ça change*," groan the exasperated French (who should certainly know), "*plus c'est le même chose*." (The more it changes, the more it remains the same.) At least they have the style to be truthful about it.

The only real change vividly discernible in this present, unspeakably dangerous chaos is a panic-stricken apprehension on the part of those who have maligned and subjugated others for so long that the tables have been turned. Not once have the Civilized been able to honor, recognize, or describe the Savage. He is, practically speaking, the source of their wealth, his continued subjugation the key to their power and glory. This is absolutely and unanswerably true in South Africa—to name but one section of Africa—and, as to how things fare for Black men and women; here, the Black has become, economically, all but expendable and is, therefore, encouraged to join the Army, or, a notion espoused, I believe, by Daniel Moynihan and Nathan Glazer, to become a post-man—to make himself useful, for Christ's sake, while White men take on the heavy burden of ruling the world.

Well. *Plus ça change.* To say nothing, speaking as a Black citizen, regarding his countrymen, of *friends like these.*

There is an unadmitted icy panic coiled beneath the scaffolding of these present days, hopes, endeavors. I have said that the Civilized have never been able to honor, recognize, or describe the Savage. Once they had decided that he was savage, there was nothing to honor, recognize or describe. But the savages describe the Europeans, who were not yet, when they landed in the New (!) World, White, as *the people from heaven.* Neither did the savages in Africa have any way of foreseeing the anguished diaspora to which they were about to be condemned. Even the chiefs who sold Africans into slavery could not have had any idea that this slavery was meant to endure forever, or for at least *a thousand years.* Nothing in the savage experience could have prepared them for such an idea, any more than they could conceive of the land as something to be bought and sold. (As I cannot believe that people are actually buying and selling air space above the towers of Manhattan.)

Nevertheless, all of this happened, and is happening. Out of this incredible brutality, we get the myth of the happy darky and *Gone With the Wind*. And the North Americans appear to believe these legends, which they have created and which absolutely nothing in reality corroborates, until today. And when these legends are attacked, as is happening now—all over a globe which has never been and never will be White—my countrymen become childishly vindictive and unutterably dangerous.

The unadmitted panic of which I spoke above is created by the terror that the Savage can, now, describe the Civilized: the only way to prevent this is to obliterate humanity. This panic proves that neither a person nor a people can do anything without knowing what they are doing. Neither can anyone avoid paying for the choices he or she has made. It is savagely, if one may say so, ironical that the only proof the world—mankind—has ever had of White supremacy is in the Black face and voice: that face never scrutinized, that voice never heard. The eyes in that face prove the unforgivable and unimaginable horror of being a captive in the promised land, but also prove that *trouble don't last always:* and the voice, once filled with a rage and pain that corroborated the reality of the jailer, is addressing another reality, in other tongues. The people who think of themselves as White have the choice of becoming human or irrelevant.

Or—as they are, indeed, already, in all but actual fact: obsolete. For, if trouble don't last always, as the Preacher tells us, neither does Power, and it is on the fact or the hope or the myth of Power that that identity which calls itself White has always seemed to depend.

I had just turned thirty-one when this book was first published, and, by the time you read this, I will be sixty. I think that quite remarkable, but I do not mention it, now, as an occasion for celebrations or lamentations. I don't feel that I have any reason to complain: emphatically, the contrary, to leave it at that, and no matter what tomorrow brings. Yet, I have reason to reflect—one always does, when forced to take a long look back. I remember many people who helped me in indescribable ways, all those years ago, when I was the popeyed, tongue-tied kid, in my memory sitting in a corner, on the floor. I was having a rough time in the Village, where the bulk of the populace, egged on by the cops, thought it was great fun to bounce tables and chairs off my head, and I soon stopped talking about my "constitutional" rights. I am, I suppose, a survivor.

A survivor of what? In those years, I was told, when I became terrified, vehement, or lachrymose: *It takes time, Jimmy. It takes time.* I agree: I still agree: though it certainly didn't take much time for some of the people I knew then— in the Fifties—to turn tail, to decide to make it, and drape themselves in the American flag. A wretched and despicable band of cowards, whom I once trusted with my life—*friends like these!*

But we will discuss all that another day. When I was told, it takes time, when I was young, I was being told it will take time before a Black person can be treated as a human being here, but it will happen. We will help to make it happen. We promise you.

Sixty years of one man's life is a long time to deliver on a promise, especially considering all the lives preceding and surrounding my own.

What has happened, in the time of my time, is the record of my ancestors. No promise was kept with them, no promise was kept with me, nor can I counsel those coming after me, nor my global kinsmen, to believe a word uttered by my morally bankrupt and desperately dishonest countrymen.

"*And,*" says Doris Lessing, in her preface to *African Stories, "while the cruelties of the white man toward the black man are among the heaviest counts in the indictment against humanity, colour prejudice is not our original fault, but only one aspect of the atrophy of the imagination that prevents us from seeing ourselves in every creature that breathes under the sun.*"

Amen. *En avant.*

18 April 1984
Amherst, Massachusetts

NOTES OF A NATIVE SON

Autobiographical Notes

I was born in Harlem thirty-one years ago. I began plotting novels at about the time I learned to read. The story of my childhood is the usual bleak fantasy, and we can dismiss it with the restrained observation that I certainly would not consider living it again. In those days my mother was given to the exasperating and mysterious habit of having babies. As they were born, I took them over with one hand and held a book with the other. The children probably suffered, though they have since been kind enough to deny it, and in this way I read *Uncle Tom's Cabin* and *A Tale of Two Cities* over and over and over again; in this way, in fact, I read just about everything I could get my hands on—except the Bible, probably because it was the only book I was encouraged to read. I must also confess that I wrote—a great deal—and my first professional triumph, in any case, the first effort of mine to be seen in print, occurred at the age of twelve or thereabouts, when a short story I had written about the Spanish revolution won some sort of prize in an extremely short-lived church newspaper. I remember the story was censored by the lady editor, though I don't remember why, and I was outraged.

Also wrote plays, and songs, for one of which I received a letter of congratulations from Mayor La Guardia, and poetry, about which the less said, the better. My mother was delighted by all these goings-on, but my father wasn't; he wanted me to be a preacher. When I was fourteen I became a preacher, and when I was seventeen I stopped. Very shortly thereafter I left home. For God knows how long I struggled with the world of commerce and industry—I guess they would say they struggled with *me*—and when I was about twenty-one I had enough done of a novel to get a Saxton Fellowship. When I was twenty-two the fellowship was over, the novel turned out to be unsalable, and I started waiting on tables in a Village restaurant and writing book reviews—mostly, as it turned out, about the Negro problem, concerning which the color of my skin made me automatically an expert. Did another book, in company with photographer Theodore Pelatowski, about the store-front churches in Harlem. This book met exactly the same fate as my first—fellowship, but no sale. (It was a Rosenwald Fellowship.) By the time I was twenty-four I had decided to stop reviewing books about the Negro problem—which, by this time, was only slightly less horrible in print than it was in life—and I packed my bags and went to France, where I finished, God knows how, *Go Tell It on the Mountain*.

Any writer, I suppose, feels that the world into which he was born is nothing less than a conspiracy against the cultivation of his talent—which attitude certainly has a great deal to support it. On the other hand, it is only because the world looks on his talent with such a frightening indifference that the artist is compelled to make his talent important. So that any writer, looking back over even so short a span of time as I am here forced to assess, finds that the things which hurt him and the things which helped him cannot be divorced from each other; he could be helped in a certain way only because he was hurt in a certain way; and his help is simply to be enabled to move from one conundrum to the next—one is tempted to say that he moves from one disaster to the next. When one begins looking for influences one finds them by the score. I haven't thought much about my own, not enough anyway; I hazard that the King James Bible, the rhetoric of the store-front church, something ironic and violent and perpetually understated in Negro speech—and something of Dickens' love for bravura—have something to do with me today; but I wouldn't stake my life on it. Likewise, innumerable people have helped me in many ways; but finally, I suppose, the most difficult (and most rewarding) thing in my life has been the fact that I was born a Negro and was forced, therefore, to effect some kind of truce with this reality. (Truce, by the way, is the best one can hope for.)

One of the difficulties about being a Negro writer (and this is not special pleading, since I don't mean to suggest that he has it worse than anybody else) is that the Negro problem is written about so widely. The bookshelves groan under the weight of information, and everyone therefore considers himself informed. And this information, furthermore, operates usually (generally, popularly) to reinforce traditional attitudes. Of traditional attitudes there are only two—For or Against—and I, personally, find it difficult to say which attitude has caused me the most pain. I am speaking as a writer; from a social point of view I am perfectly aware that the change from ill-will to good-will, however motivated, however imperfect, however expressed, is better than no change at all.

But it is part of the business of the writer—as I see it—
to examine attitudes, to go beneath the surface, to tap the
source. From this point of view the Negro problem is nearly
inaccessible. It is not only written about so widely; it is written about so badly. It is quite possible to say that the price
a Negro pays for becoming articulate is to find himself, at
length, with nothing to be articulate about. ("You taught
me language," says Caliban to Prospero, "and my profit on't
is I know how to curse.") Consider: the tremendous social
activity that this problem generates imposes on whites and
Negroes alike the necessity of looking forward, of working
to bring about a better day. This is fine, it keeps the waters
troubled; it is all, indeed, that has made possible the Negro's
progress. Nevertheless, social affairs are not generally speaking the writer's prime concern, whether they ought to be or
not; it is absolutely necessary that he establish between himself and these affairs a distance which will allow, at least, for
clarity, so that before he can look forward in any meaningful
sense, he must first be allowed to take a long look back. In
the context of the Negro problem neither whites nor blacks,
for excellent reasons of their own, have the faintest desire to
look back; but I think that the past is all that makes the present coherent, and further, that the past will remain horrible
for exactly as long as we refuse to assess it honestly.

I know, in any case, that the most crucial time in my own
development came when I was forced to recognize that I was
a kind of bastard of the West; when I followed the line of my
past I did not find myself in Europe but in Africa. And this
meant that in some subtle way, in a really profound way, I
brought to Shakespeare, Bach, Rembrandt, to the stones of
Paris, to the cathedral at Chartres, and to the Empire State

Building, a special attitude. These were not really my creations, they did not contain my history; I might search in them in vain forever for any reflection of myself. I was an interloper; this was not my heritage. At the same time I had no other heritage which I could possibly hope to use—I had certainly been unfitted for the jungle or the tribe. I would have to appropriate these white centuries, I would have to make them mine—I would have to accept my special attitude, my special place in this scheme—otherwise I would have no place in *any* scheme. What was the most difficult was the fact that I was forced to admit something I had always hidden from myself, which the American Negro has had to hide from himself as the price of his public progress; that I hated and feared white people. This did not mean that I loved black people; on the contrary, I despised them, possibly because they failed to produce Rembrandt. In effect, I hated and feared the world. And this meant, not only that I thus gave the world an altogether murderous power over me, but also that in such a self-destroying limbo I could never hope to write.

One writes out of one thing only—one's own experience. Everything depends on how relentlessly one forces from this experience the last drop, sweet or bitter, it can possibly give. This is the only real concern of the artist, to recreate out of the disorder of life that order which is art. The difficulty then, for me, of being a Negro writer was the fact that I was, in effect, prohibited from examining my own experience too closely by the tremendous demands and the very real dangers of my social situation.

I don't think the dilemma outlined above is uncommon. I do think, since writers work in the disastrously explicit medium of language, that it goes a little way towards explaining why, out of the enormous resources of Negro speech and life, and despite the example of Negro music, prose written by Negroes has been generally speaking so pallid and so harsh. I have not written about being a Negro at such length because I expect that to be my only subject, but only because it was the gate I had to unlock before I could hope to write about anything else. I don't think that the Negro problem in America can be even discussed coherently without bearing in mind its context; its context being the history, traditions, customs, the moral assumptions and preoccupations of the country; in short, the general social fabric. Appearances to the contrary, no one in America escapes its effects and everyone in America bears some responsibility for it. I believe this the more firmly because it is the overwhelming tendency to speak of this problem as though it were a thing apart. But in the work of Faulkner, in the general attitude and certain specific passages in Robert Penn Warren, and, most significantly, in the advent of Ralph Ellison, one sees the beginnings—at least—of a more genuinely penetrating search. Mr. Ellison, by the way, is the first Negro novelist I have ever read to utilize in language, and brilliantly, some of the ambiguity and irony of Negro life.

About my interests: I don't know if I have any, unless the morbid desire to own a sixteen-millimeter camera and make experimental movies can be so classified. Otherwise, I love to eat and drink—it's my melancholy conviction that I've scarcely ever had enough to eat (this is because it's *impossible* to eat enough if you're worried about the next meal)—and I love to argue with people who do not disagree with me too profoundly, and I love to laugh. I do *not* like bohemia, or bohemians, I do not like people whose principal aim is pleasure, and I do not like people who are *earnest* about anything. I don't like people who like me because I'm a Negro; neither do I like people who find in the same accident grounds for contempt. I love America more than any other country in the world, and, exactly for this reason, I insist on the right to criticize her perpetually. I think all theories are suspect, that the finest principles may have to be modified, or may even be pulverized by the demands of life, and that one must find, therefore, one's own moral center and move through the world hoping that this center will guide one aright. I consider that I have many responsibilities, but none greater than this: to last, as Hemingway says, and get my work done.

I want to be an honest man and a good writer.

PART ONE

Everybody's Protest Novel

In *Uncle Tom's Cabin,* that cornerstone of American social protest fiction, St. Clare, the kindly master, remarks to his coldly disapproving Yankee cousin, Miss Ophelia, that, so far as he is able to tell, the blacks have been turned over to the devil for the benefit of the whites in this world—however, he adds thoughtfully, it may turn out in the next. Miss Ophelia's reaction is, at least, vehemently right-minded: "This is perfectly horrible!" she exclaims. "You ought to be ashamed of yourselves!"

Miss Ophelia, as we may suppose, was speaking for the author; her exclamation is the moral, neatly framed, and incontestable like those improving mottoes sometimes found hanging on the walls of furnished rooms. And, like these mottoes, before which one invariably flinches, recognizing an insupportable, almost an indecent glibness, she and St. Clare are terribly in earnest. Neither of them questions the medieval morality from which their dialogue springs: black, white, the devil, the next world—posing its alternatives between heaven and the flames—were realities for them as, of course, they were for their creator. They spurned and were terrified of the darkness, striving mightily for the light; and considered from this aspect, Miss Ophelia's exclamation, like Mrs. Stowe's novel, achieves a bright, almost a lurid significance, like the light from a fire which consumes a witch. This is the more striking as one considers the novels of Negro oppression written in our own, more enlightened day, all of which say only: "This is perfectly horrible! You ought to be ashamed of yourselves!" (Let us ignore, for the moment, those novels of oppression written by Negroes, which add only a raging, near-paranoiac postscript to this statement and actually reinforce, as I hope to make clear later, the principles which activate the oppression they decry.)

Uncle Tom's Cabin is a very bad novel, having, in its self-righteous, virtuous sentimentality, much in common with Little Women. Sentimentality, the ostentatious parading of excessive and spurious emotion, is the mark of dishonesty, the inability to feel; the wet eyes of the sentimentalist betray his aversion to experience, his fear of life, his arid heart; and it is always, therefore, the signal of secret and violent inhumanity, the mask of cruelty. Uncle Tom's Cabin—like its multitudinous, hard-boiled descendants—is a catalogue of violence. This is explained by the nature of Mrs. Stowe's subject matter, her laudable determination to flinch from nothing in presenting the complete picture; an explanation which falters only if we pause to ask whether or not her picture is indeed complete; and what constriction or failure of perception forced her to so depend on the description of brutality—unmotivated, senseless—and to leave unanswered and unnoticed the only important question: what it was, after all, that moved her people to such deeds.

But this, let us say, was beyond Mrs. Stowe's powers; she was not so much a novelist as an impassioned pamphleteer;

her book was not intended to do anything more than prove that slavery was wrong; was, in fact, perfectly horrible. This makes material for a pamphlet but it is hardly enough for a novel; and the only question left to ask is why we are bound still within the same constriction. How is it that we are so loath to make a further journey than that made by Mrs. Stowe, to discover and reveal something a little closer to the truth?

But that battered word, truth, having made its appearance here, confronts one immediately with a series of riddles and has, moreover, since so many gospels are preached, the unfortunate tendency to make one belligerent. Let us say, then, that truth, as used here, is meant to imply a devotion to the human being, his freedom and fulfillment; freedom which cannot be legislated, fulfillment which cannot be charted. This is the prime concern, the frame of reference; it is not to be confused with a devotion to Humanity which is too easily equated with a devotion to a Cause; and Causes, as we know, are notoriously bloodthirsty. We have, as it seems to me, in this most mechanical and interlocking of civilizations, attempted to lop this creature down to the status of a time-saving invention. He is not, after all, merely a member of a Society or a Group or a deplorable conundrum to be explained by Science. He is—and how old-fashioned the words sound!—something more than that, something resolutely indefinable, unpredictable. In overlooking, denying, evading his complexity—which is nothing more than the disquieting complexity of ourselves—we are diminished and we perish; only within this web of ambiguity, paradox, this hunger, danger, darkness, can we find at once ourselves and the power that will free us from ourselves. It is this power of revelation which is the business of the novelist, this journey toward a more vast reality which must take precedence over all other claims. What is today parroted as his Responsibility—which seems to mean that he must make formal declaration that he is involved in, and affected by, the lives of other people and to say something improving about this somewhat self-evident fact—is, when he believes it, his corruption and our loss; moreover, it is rooted in, interlocked with and intensifies this same mechanization. Both *Gentleman's Agreement* and *The Postman Always Rings Twice* exemplify this terror of the human being, the determination to cut him down to size. And in *Uncle Tom's Cabin* we may find foreshadowing of both: the formula created by the necessity to find a lie more palatable than the truth has been handed down and memorized and persists yet with a terrible power.

It is interesting to consider one more aspect of Mrs. Stowe's novel, the method she used to solve the problem of writing about a black man at all. Apart from her lively procession of field hands, house niggers, Chloe, Topsy, etc.—who are the stock, lovable figures presenting no problem—she has only three other Negroes in the book. These are the important ones and two of them may be dismissed immediately, since we have only the author's word that they are Negro and they are, in all other respects, as white as she can make them. The two are George and Eliza, a married couple with a wholly adorable child—whose quaintness, incidentally, and whose charm, rather put one in mind of a darky bootblack doing a buck and wing to the clatter of condescending coins. Eliza is a beautiful, pious hybrid, light enough to pass—the heroine of *Quality* might, indeed, be her reincarnation—differing from the genteel mistress who has overseered her education only in the respect that she is a servant. George is darker, but makes up for it by being a mechanical genius, and is, moreover, sufficiently un-Negroid to pass through town, a fugitive from his master, disguised as a Spanish gentleman, attracting no attention whatever beyond admiration. They are a race apart from Topsy. It transpires by the end of the novel, through one of those energetic, last-minute convolutions of the plot, that Eliza has some connection with French gentility. The figure from whom the novel takes its name, Uncle Tom, who is a figure of controversy yet, is jet-black, wooly-haired, illiterate; and he is phenomenally forbearing. He has to be; he is black; only through this forbearance can he survive or triumph. (*Cf.* Faulkner's preface to *The Sound and the Fury*: These others were not Compsons. They were black:—They endured.) His triumph is metaphysical, unearthly; since he is black, born without the light, it is only through humility, the incessant mortification of the flesh, that he can enter into communion with God or man. The virtuous rage of Mrs. Stowe is motivated by nothing so temporal as a concern for the relationship of men to one another—or, even, as she would have claimed, by a concern for their relationship to God—but merely by a panic of being hurled into the flames, of being caught in traffic with the devil. She embraced this merciless doctrine with all her heart, bargaining shamelessly before the throne of grace: God and salvation becoming her personal property, purchased with the coin of her virtue. Here, black equates with evil and white with grace; if, being mindful of the necessity of good works, she could not cast out the blacks—a wretched, huddled mass, apparently, claiming, like an obsession, her inner eye—she could not embrace them either without purifying them of sin. She must cover their intimidating nakedness, robe them

in white, the garments of salvation; only thus could she herself be delivered from ever-present sin, only thus could she
bury, as St. Paul demanded, "the carnal man, the man of the
flesh." Tom, therefore, her only black man, has been robbed
of his humanity and divested of his sex. It is the price for that
darkness with which he has been branded.

Uncle Tom's Cabin, then, is activated by what might be
called a theological terror, the terror of damnation; and the
spirit that breathes in this book, hot, self-righteous, fearful, is
not different from that spirit of medieval times which sought
to exorcize evil by burning witches; and is not different from
that terror which activates a lynch mob. One need not, indeed, search for examples so historic or so gaudy; this is a
warfare waged daily in the heart, a warfare so vast, so relent-
less and so powerful that the interracial handshake or the interracial marriage can be as crucifying as the public hanging
or the secret rape. This panic motivates our cruelty, this fear
of the dark makes it impossible that our lives shall be other
than superficial; this, interlocked with and feeding our glittering, mechanical, inescapable civilization which has put to
death our freedom.

This, notwithstanding that the avowed aim of the American protest novel is to bring greater freedom to the oppressed. They are forgiven, on the strength of these good
intentions, whatever violence they do to language, whatever
excessive demands they make of credibility. It is, indeed,
considered the sign of a frivolity so intense as to approach
decadence to suggest that these books are both badly written
and wildly improbable. One is told to put first things first, the
good of society coming before niceties of style or character-
ization. Even if this were incontestable—for what exactly is

the "good" of society?—it argues an insuperable confusion, since literature and sociology are not one and the same; it is impossible to discuss them as if they were. Our passion for categorization, life neatly fitted into pegs, has led to an unforeseen, paradoxical distress; confusion, a breakdown of meaning. Those categories which were meant to define and control the world for us have boomeranged us into chaos; in which limbo we whirl, clutching the straws of our definitions. The "protest" novel, so far from being disturbing, is an accepted and comforting aspect of the American scene, ramifying that framework we believe to be so necessary. Whatever unsettling questions are raised are evanescent, titillating; remote, for this has nothing to do with us, it is safely ensconced in the social arena, where, indeed, it has nothing to do with anyone, so that finally we receive a very definite thrill of virtue from the fact that we are reading such a book at all. This report from the pit reassures us of its reality and its darkness and of our own salvation; and "As long as such books are being published," an American liberal once said to me, "everything will be all right."

But unless one's ideal of society is a race of neatly analyzed, hard-working ciphers, one can hardly claim for the protest novels the lofty purpose they claim for themselves or share the present optimism concerning them. They emerge for what they are: a mirror of our confusion, dishonesty, panic, trapped and immobilized in the sunlit prison of the American dream. They are fantasies, connecting nowhere with reality, sentimental; in exactly the same sense that such movies as *The Best Years of Our Lives* or the works of Mr. James M. Cain are fantasies. Beneath the dazzling pyrotechnics of these current operas one may still discern, as the controlling force, the intense theological preoccupations of Mrs. Stowe, the sick vacuities of *The Rover Boys*. Finally, the aim of the protest novel becomes something very closely resembling the zeal of those alabaster missionaries to Africa to cover the nakedness of the natives, to hurry them into the pallid arms of Jesus and thence into slavery. The aim has now become to reduce all Americans to the compulsive, bloodless dimensions of a guy named Joe.

It is the peculiar triumph of society—and its loss—that it is able to convince those people to whom it has given inferior status of the reality of this decree; it has the force and the weapons to translate its dictum into fact, so that the allegedly inferior are actually made so, insofar as the societal realities are concerned. This is a more hidden phenomenon now than it was in the days of serfdom, but it is no less implacable. Now, as then, we find ourselves bound, first without, then within, by the nature of our categorization. And escape is not effected through a bitter railing against this trap; it is as though this very striving were the only motion needed to spring the trap upon us. We take our shape, it is true, within and against that cage of reality bequeathed us at our birth; and yet it is precisely through our dependence on this reality that we are most endlessly betrayed. Society is held together by our need; we bind it together with legend, myth, coercion, fearing that without it we will be hurled into that void, within which, like the earth before the Word was spoken, the foundations of society are hidden. From this void—ourselves—it is the function of society to protect us; but it is only this void, our unknown selves, demanding, forever, a new act of creation, which can save us—"from the evil that is in the world." With the same motion, at the same time, it is this toward which we endlessly struggle and from which, endlessly, we struggle to escape.

It must be remembered that the oppressed and the oppressor are bound together within the same society; they accept the same criteria, they share the same beliefs, they both alike depend on the same reality. Within this cage it is romantic, more, meaningless, to speak of a "new" society as the desire of the oppressed, for that shivering dependence on the props of reality which he shares with the *Herrenvolk* makes a truly "new" society impossible to conceive. What is meant by a new society is one in which inequalities will disappear, in which vengeance will be exacted; either there will be no oppressed at all, or the oppressed and the oppressor will change places. But, finally, as it seems to me, what the rejected desire is, is an elevation of status, acceptance within the present community. Thus, the African, exile, pagan, hurried off the auction block and into the fields, fell on his knees before that God in Whom he must now believe; who had made him, but not in His image. This tableau, this impossibility, is the heritage of the Negro in America: *Wash me, cried the slave to his Maker, and I shall be whiter, whiter than snow!* For black is the color of evil; only the robes of the saved are white. It is this cry, implacable on the air and in the skull, that he must live with. Beneath the widely published catalogue of brutality—bringing to mind, somehow, an image, a memory of church-bells burdening the air—is this reality which, in the same nightmare notion, he both flees and rushes to embrace. In America, now, this country devoted to the death of the paradox—which may, therefore, be put to death by one—his lot is as ambiguous as a tableau by Kafka. To flee or not, to move or not, it is all the same; his doom is written on his forehead, it is carried in his heart. In *Native Son,* Bigger Thomas stands on a Chicago street corner watching airplanes flown by white men racing against the sun and "Goddamn" he says, the bitterness bubbling up like blood, remembering a million indignities, the terrible, rat-infested house, the humiliation of home-relief, the intense, aimless, ugly bickering, hating it; hatred smoulders through these pages like sulphur fire. All of Bigger's life is controlled, defined by his hatred and his fear. And later, his fear drives him to murder and his hatred to rape; he dies, having come, through this violence, we are told, for the first time, to a kind of life, having for the first time redeemed his manhood. Below the surface of this novel there lies, as it seems to me, a continuation, a complement of that monstrous legend it was written to destroy. Bigger is Uncle Tom's descendant, flesh of his flesh, so exactly opposite a portrait that, when the books are placed together, it seems that the contemporary Negro novelist and the dead New England woman are locked together in a deadly, timeless battle; the one uttering merciless exhortations, the other shouting curses. And, indeed, within this web of lust and fury, black and white can only thrust and counter-thrust, long for each other's slow, exquisite death; death by torture, acid, knives and burning; the thrust, the counter-thrust, the longing making the heavier that cloud which blinds and suffocates them both, so that they go down into the pit together. Thus has the cage betrayed us all, this moment, our life, turned to nothing through our terrible attempts to insure it. For Bigger's tragedy is not that he is cold or black or hungry, not even that he is American, black; but that he has accepted a theology that denies him life, that he admits the possibility of his being sub-human and feels constrained, therefore, to battle for his humanity according to those brutal criteria bequeathed him at his birth. But our humanity is our burden, our life; we need not battle for it; we need only to do what is infinitely more difficult—that is, accept it. The failure of the protest novel lies in its rejection of life, the human being, the denial of his beauty, dread, power, in its insistence that it is his categorization alone which is real and which cannot be transcended.

Many Thousands Gone

It is only in his music, which Americans are able to admire because a protective sentimentality limits their understanding of it, that the Negro in America has been able to tell his story. It is a story which otherwise has yet to be told and which no American is prepared to hear. As is the inevitable result of things unsaid, we find ourselves until today oppressed with a dangerous and reverberating silence; and the story is told, compulsively, in symbols and signs, in hieroglyphics; it is revealed in Negro speech and in that of the white majority and in their different frames of reference. The ways in which the Negro has affected the American psychology are betrayed in our popular culture and in our morality; in our estrangement from him is the depth of our estrangement from ourselves. We cannot ask: what do we *really* feel about him—such a question merely opens the gates on chaos. What we really feel about him is involved with all that we feel about everything, about everyone, about ourselves.

The story of the Negro in America is the story of America—or, more precisely, it is the story of Americans. It is not a very pretty story: the story of a people is never very pretty. The Negro in America, gloomily referred to as that shadow which lies athwart our national life, is far more than that. He is a series of shadows, self-created, intertwining, which now we helplessly battle. One may say that the Negro in America does not really exist except in the darkness of our minds.

This is why his history and his progress, his relationship to all other Americans, has been kept in the social arena. He is a social and not a personal or a human problem; to think of him is to think of statistics, slums, rapes, injustices, remote violence; it is to be confronted with an endless cataloguing of losses, gains, skirmishes; it is to feel virtuous, outraged, helpless, as though his continuing status among us were somehow analogous to disease—cancer, perhaps, or tuberculosis—which must be checked, even though it cannot be cured. In this arena the black man acquires quite another aspect from that which he has in life. We do not know what to do with him in life; if he breaks our sociological and sentimental image of him we are panic-stricken and we feel ourselves betrayed. When he violates this image, therefore, he stands in the greatest danger (sensing which, we uneasily suspect that he is very often playing a part for our benefit); and, what is not always so apparent but is equally true, we are then in some danger ourselves—hence our retreat or our blind and immediate retaliation.

Our dehumanization of the Negro then is indivisible from our dehumanization of ourselves: the loss of our own identity is the price we pay for our annulment of his. Time and our own force act as our allies, creating an impossible, a fruitless tension between the traditional master and slave. Impossible and fruitless because, literal and visible as this tension has become, it has nothing to do with reality.

Time has made some changes in the Negro face. Nothing has succeeded in making it exactly like our own, though the general desire seems to be to make it blank if one cannot make it white. When it has become blank, the past as thoroughly washed from the black face as it has been from ours, our guilt will be finished—at least it will have ceased to be visible, which we imagine to be much the same thing. But, paradoxically, it is we who prevent this from happening; since it is we, who, every hour that we live, reinvest the black face with our guilt; and we do this—by a further paradox, no less ferocious—helplessly, passionately, out of an unrealized need to suffer absolution.

Today, to be sure, we know that the Negro is not biologically or mentally inferior; there is no truth in those rumors of his body odor or his incorrigible sexuality; or no more truth than can be easily explained or even defended by the social sciences. Yet, in our most recent war, his blood was segregated as was, for the most part, his person. Up to today we are set at a division, so that he may not marry our daughters or our sisters, nor may he—for the most part—eat at our tables or live in our houses. Moreover, those who do, do so at the grave expense of a double alienation: from their own people, whose fabled attributes they must either deny or, worse, cheapen and bring to market; from us, for we require of them, when we accept them, that they at once cease to be Negroes and yet not fail to remember what being a Negro means—to remember, that is, what it means to us. The threshold of insult is higher or lower, according to the people involved, from the bootblack in Atlanta to the celebrity in New York. One must travel very far, among saints with nothing to gain or outcasts

with nothing to lose, to find a place where it does not matter—and perhaps a word or a gesture or simply a silence will
testify that it matters even there.

For it means something to be a Negro, after all, as it
means something to have been born in Ireland or in China,
to live where one sees space and sky or to live where one sees
nothing but rubble or nothing but high buildings. We cannot
escape our origins, however hard we try, those origins which
contain the key—could we but find it—to all that we later
become. What it means to be a Negro is a good deal more
than this essay can discover; what it means to be a Negro in
America can perhaps be suggested by an examination of the
myths we perpetuate about him.

Aunt Jemima and Uncle Tom are dead, their places
taken by a group of amazingly well-adjusted young men and
women, almost as dark, but ferociously literate, well-dressed
and scrubbed, who are never laughed at, who are not likely
ever to set foot in a cotton or tobacco field or in any but the
most modern of kitchens. There are others who remain, in
our odd idiom, "underprivileged"; some are bitter and these
come to grief; some are unhappy, but, continually presented
with the evidence of a better day soon to come, are speedily
becoming less so. Most of them care nothing whatever about
race. They want only their proper place in the sun and the
right to be left alone, like any other citizen of the republic.
We may all breathe more easily. Before, however, our joy at
the demise of Aunt Jemima and Uncle Tom approaches the
indecent, we had better ask whence they sprang, how they
lived? Into what limbo have they vanished?

However inaccurate our portraits of them were, these portraits do suggest, not only the conditions, but the quality of

their lives and the impact of this spectacle on our consciences. There was no one more forbearing than Aunt Jemima, no one stronger or more pious or more loyal or more wise; there was, at the same time, no one weaker or more faithless or more vicious and certainly no one more immoral. Uncle Tom, trustworthy and sexless, needed only to drop the title "Uncle" to become violent, crafty, and sullen, a menace to any white woman who passed by. They prepared our feast tables and our burial clothes; and, if we could boast that we understood them, it was far more to the point and far more true that they understood us. They were, moreover, the only people in the world who did; and not only did they know us better than we knew ourselves, but they knew us better than we knew them. This was the piquant flavoring to the national joke, it lay behind our uneasiness as it lay behind our benevolence: Aunt Jemima and Uncle Tom, our creations, at the last evaded us; they had a life—their own, perhaps a better life than ours—and they would never tell us what it was. At the point where we were driven most privately and painfully to conjecture what depths of contempt, what heights of indifference, what prodigies of resilience, what untamable superiority allowed them so vividly to endure, neither perishing nor rising up in a body to wipe us from the earth, the image perpetually shattered and the word failed. The black man in our midst carried murder in his heart, he wanted vengeance. We carried murder too, we wanted peace.

In our image of the Negro breathes the past we deny, not dead but living yet and powerful, the beast in our jungle of statistics. It is this which defeats us, which continues to defeat us, which lends to interracial cocktail parties their rattling, genteel, nervously smiling air: in any drawing room at

such a gathering the beast may spring, filling the air with flying things and an unenlightened wailing. Wherever the problem touches there is confusion, there is danger. Wherever
the Negro face appears a tension is created, the tension of a
silence filled with things unutterable. It is a sentimental er-
ror, therefore, to believe that the past is dead; it means nothing to say that it is all forgotten, that the Negro himself has
forgotten it. It is not a question of memory. Oedipus did not
remember the thongs that bound his feet; nevertheless the
marks they left testified to that doom toward which his feet
were leading him. The man does not remember the hand
that struck him, the darkness that frightened him, as a child;
nevertheless, the hand and the darkness remain with him, indivisible from himself forever, part of the passion that drives
him wherever he thinks to take flight.

The making of an American begins at that point where he
himself rejects all other ties, any other history, and himself
adopts the vesture of his adopted land. This problem has been
faced by all Americans throughout our history—in a way it *is*
our history—and it baffles the immigrant and sets on edge
the second generation until today. In the case of the Negro
the past was taken from him whether he would or no; yet to
forswear it was meaningless and availed him nothing, since
his shameful history was carried, quite literally, on his brow.
Shameful; for he was heathen as well as black and would
never have discovered the healing blood of Christ had not we
braved the jungles to bring him these glad tidings. Shameful;
for, since our role as missionary had not been wholly disinter-
ested, it was necessary to recall the shame from which we had

delivered him in order more easily to escape our own. As he accepted the alabaster Christ and the bloody cross—in the bearing of which he would find his redemption, as, indeed, to our outraged astonishment, he sometimes did—he must, henceforth, accept that image we then gave him of himself: having no other and standing, moreover, in danger of death should he fail to accept the dazzling light thus brought into such darkness. It is this quite simple dilemma that must be borne in mind if we wish to comprehend his psychology.

However we shift the light which beats so fiercely on his head, or *prove,* by victorious social analysis, how his lot has changed, how we have both improved, our uneasiness refuses to be exorcized. And nowhere is this more apparent than in our literature on the subject—"problem" literature when written by whites, "protest" literature when written by Negroes— and nothing is more striking than the tremendous disparity of tone between the two creations. *Kingsblood Royal* bears, for example, almost no kinship to *If He Hollers Let Him Go,* though the same reviewers praised them both for what were, at bottom, very much the same reasons. These reasons may be suggested, far too briefly but not at all unjustly, by observing that the presupposition is in both novels exactly the same: black is a terrible color with which to be born into the world.

Now the most powerful and celebrated statement we have yet had of what it means to be a Negro in America is unquestionably Richard Wright's *Native Son.* The feeling which prevailed at the time of its publication was that such a novel, bitter, uncompromising, shocking, gave proof, by its very existence, of what strides might be taken in a free democracy; and its indisputable success, proof that Americans were now able to look full in the face without flinching the dreadful facts. Americans, unhappily, have the most remarkable ability to alchemize all bitter truths into an innocuous but piquant confection and to transform their moral contradictions, or public discussion of such contradictions, into a proud decoration, such as are given for heroism on the field of battle. Such a book, we felt with pride, could never have been written before—which was true. Nor could it be written today. It bears already the aspect of a landmark; for Bigger and his brothers have undergone yet another metamorphosis; they have been accepted in baseball leagues and by colleges hitherto exclusive; and they have made a most favorable appearance on the national screen. We have yet to encounter, nevertheless, a report so indisputably authentic, or one that can begin to challenge this most significant novel.

It is, in a certain American tradition, the story of an unremarkable youth in battle with the force of circumstance; that force of circumstance which plays and which has played so important a part in the national fables of success or failure. In this case the force of circumstance is not poverty merely but color, a circumstance which cannot be overcome, against which the protagonist battles for his life and loses. It is, on the surface, remarkable that this book should have enjoyed among Americans the favor it did enjoy; no more remarkable, however, than that it should have been compared, exuberantly, to Dostoevsky, though placed a shade below Dos Passos, Dreiser, and Steinbeck; and when the book is examined, its impact does not seem remarkable at all, but becomes, on the contrary, perfectly logical and inevitable.

We cannot, to begin with, divorce this book from the specific social climate of that time: it was one of the last of those angry productions, encountered in the late twenties and all through the thirties, dealing with the inequities of the social structure of America. It was published one year before our entry into the last world war—which is to say, very few years after the dissolution of the WPA and the end of the New Deal and at a time when bread lines and soup kitchens and bloody industrial battles were bright in everyone's memory. The rigors of that unexpected time filled us not only with a genuinely bewildered and despairing idealism—so that, because there at least was *something* to fight for, young men went off to die in Spain—but also with a genuinely bewildered self-consciousness. The Negro, who had been during the magnificent twenties a passionate and delightful primitive, now became, as one of the things we were most self-conscious about, our most oppressed minority. In the thirties, swallowing Marx whole, we discovered the Worker and realized—I should think with some relief—that the aims of the Worker and the aims of the Negro were one. This theorem—to which we shall return—seems now to leave rather too much out of account; it became, nevertheless, one of the slogans of the "class struggle" and the gospel of the New Negro.

As for this New Negro, it was Wright who became his most eloquent spokesman; and his work, from its beginning, is most clearly committed to the social struggle. Leaving aside the considerable question of what relationship precisely the artist bears to the revolutionary, the reality of man as a social being is not his only reality and that artist is strangled who is forced to deal with human beings solely in social terms; and who has, moreover, as Wright had, the necessity thrust on him of being the representative of some thirteen million people. It is a false responsibility (since writers are not congressmen) and impossible, by its nature, of fulfillment. The unlucky shepherd soon finds that, so far from being able to feed the hungry sheep, he has lost the wherewithal for his own nourishment: having not been allowed—so fearful was his burden, so present his audience!—to recreate his own experience. Further, the militant men and women of the thirties were not, upon examination, significantly emancipated from their antecedents, however bitterly they might consider themselves estranged or however gallantly they struggled to build a better world. However they might extol Russia, their concept of a better world was quite helplessly American and betrayed a certain thinness of imagination, a suspect reliance on suspect and badly digested formulae, and a positively fretful romantic haste. Finally, the relationship of the Negro to the Worker cannot be summed up, nor even greatly illuminated, by saying that their aims are one. It is true only insofar as they both desire better working conditions and useful only insofar as they unite their strength as workers to achieve these ends. Further than this we cannot in honesty go.

In this climate Wright's voice first was heard and the struggle which promised for a time to shape his work and give it purpose also fixed it in an ever more unrewarding rage. Recording his days of anger he has also nevertheless recorded, as no Negro before him had ever done, that fantasy Americans hold in their minds when they speak of the Negro: that fantastic and fearful image which we have lived with since the first slave fell beneath the lash. This is the significance of *Native Son* and also, unhappily, its overwhelming limitation.

Native Son begins with the *Brring!* of an alarm clock in the squalid Chicago tenement where Bigger and his family live.

Rats live there too, feeding off the garbage, and we first encounter Bigger in the act of killing one. One may consider
that the entire book, from that harsh *Brring!* to Bigger's
weak "Good-by" as the lawyer, Max, leaves him in the death
cell, is an extension, with the roles inverted, of this chilling
metaphor. Bigger's situation and Bigger himself exert on the
mind the same sort of fascination. The premise of the book
is, as I take it, clearly conveyed in these first pages: we are
confronting a monster created by the American republic and
we are, through being made to share his experience, to receive illumination as regards the manner of his life and to
feel both pity and horror at his awful and inevitable doom.
This is an arresting and potentially rich idea and we would
be discussing a very different novel if Wright's execution had
been more perceptive and if he had not attempted to redeem
a symbolical monster in social terms.

One may object that it was precisely Wright's intention to
create in Bigger a social symbol, revelatory of social disease
and prophetic of disaster. I think, however, that it is this assumption which we ought to examine more carefully. Bigger
has no discernible relationship to himself, to his own life,
to his own people, nor to any other people—in this respect,
perhaps, he is most American—and his force comes, not
from his significance as a social (or anti-social) unit, but from
his significance as the incarnation of a myth. It is remarkable
that, though we follow him step by step from the tenement
room to the death cell, we know as little about him when
this journey is ended as we did when it began; and, what is
even more remarkable, we know almost as little about the
social dynamic which we are to believe created him. Despite the details of slum life which we are given, I doubt that

anyone who has thought about it, disengaging himself from
sentimentality, can accept this most essential premise of the
novel for a moment. Those Negroes who surround him, on the
other hand, his hard-working mother, his ambitious sister, his
poolroom cronies, Bessie, might be considered as far richer
and far more subtle and accurate illustrations of the ways in
which Negroes are controlled in our society and the complex techniques they have evolved for their survival. We are
limited, however, to Bigger's view of them, part of a deliberate plan which might not have been disastrous if we were not
also limited to Bigger's perceptions. What this means for the
novel is that a necessary dimension has been cut away; this
dimension being the relationship that Negroes bear to one
another, that depth of involvement and unspoken recognition of shared experience which creates a way of life. What
the novel reflects—and at no point interprets—is the isolation of the Negro within his own group and the resulting
fury of impatient scorn. It is this which creates its climate
of anarchy and unmotivated and unapprehended disaster;
and it is this climate, common to most Negro protest novels,
which has led us all to believe that in Negro life there exists
no tradition, no field of manners, no possibility of ritual or
intercourse, such as may, for example, sustain the Jew even
after he has left his father's house. But the fact is not that
the Negro has no tradition but that there has as yet arrived
no sensibility sufficiently profound and tough to make this
tradition articulate. For a tradition expresses, after all, nothing more than the long and painful experience of a people; it
comes out of the battle waged to maintain their integrity or,
to put it more simply, out of their struggle to survive. When
we speak of the Jewish tradition we are speaking of centuries

of exile and persecution, of the strength which endured and the sensibility which discovered in it the high possibility of the moral victory.

This sense of how Negroes live and how they have so long endured is hidden from us in part by the very speed of the Negro's public progress, a progress so heavy with complexity, so bewildering and kaleidoscopic, that he dare not pause to conjecture on the darkness which lies behind him; and by the nature of the American psychology which, in order to apprehend or be made able to accept it, must undergo a metamorphosis so profound as to be literally unthinkable and which there is no doubt we will resist until we are compelled to achieve our own identity by the rigors of a time that has yet to come. Bigger, in the meanwhile, and all his furious kin, serve only to whet the notorious national taste for the sensational and to reinforce all that we now find it necessary to believe. It is not Bigger whom we fear, since his appearance among us makes our victory certain. It is the others, who smile, who go to church, who give no cause for complaint, whom we sometimes consider with amusement, with pity, even with affection—and in whose faces we sometimes surprise the merest arrogant hint of hatred, the faintest, withdrawn, speculative shadow of contempt—who make us uneasy; whom we cajole, threaten, flatter, fear; who to us remain unknown, though we are not (we feel with both relief and hostility and with bottomless confusion) unknown to them. It is out of our reaction to these hewers of wood and drawers of water that our image of Bigger was created.

It is this image, living yet, which we perpetually seek to evade with good works; and this image which makes of all our good works an intolerable mockery. The "nigger," black, benighted, brutal, consumed with hatred as we are consumed with guilt, cannot be thus blotted out. He stands at our shoulders when we give our maid her wages, it is his hand which we fear we are taking when struggling to communicate with the current "intelligent" Negro, his stench, as it were, which fills our mouths with salt as the monument is unveiled in honor of the latest Negro leader. Each generation has shouted behind him, *Nigger!* as he walked our streets; it is he whom we would rather our sisters did not marry; he is banished into the vast and wailing outer darkness whenever we speak of the "purity" of our women, of the "sanctity" of our homes, of "American" ideals. What is more, he knows it. He is indeed the "native son": he is the "nigger." Let us refrain from inquiring at the moment whether or not he actually exists; for we *believe* that he exists. Whenever we encounter him amongst us in the flesh, our faith is made perfect and his necessary and bloody end is executed with a mystical ferocity of joy.

But there is a complementary faith among the damned which involves their gathering of the stones with which those who walk in the light shall stone them; or there exists among the intolerably degraded the perverse and powerful desire to force into the arena of the actual those fantastic crimes of which they have been accused, achieving their vengeance and their own destruction through making the nightmare real. The American image of the Negro lives also in the Negro's heart; and when he has surrendered to this image life has no other possible reality. Then he, like the white enemy with whom he will be locked one day in mortal struggle, has no means save this of asserting his identity. This is why Bigger's murder of Mary can be referred to as an "act of creation" and why, once this murder has been committed, he can feel for the first time that he is living fully and deeply as a man was meant to live. And there is, I should think, no Negro living in America who has not felt, briefly or for long periods, with anguish sharp or dull, in varying degrees and to varying effect, simple, naked and unanswerable hatred; who has not wanted to smash any white face he may encounter in a day, to violate, out of motives of the cruelest vengeance, their women, to break the bodies of all white people and bring them low, as low as that dust into which he himself has been and is being trampled; no Negro, finally, who has not had to make his own precarious adjustment to the "nigger" who surrounds him and to the "nigger" in himself.

Yet the adjustment must be made—rather, it must be attempted, the tension perpetually sustained—for without this he has surrendered his birthright as a man no less than his birthright as a black man. The entire universe is then peopled only with his enemies, who are not only white men armed with rope and rifle, but his own far-flung and contemptible kinsmen. Their blackness is his degradation and it is their stupid and passive endurance which makes his end inevitable.

Bigger dreams of some black man who will weld all blacks together into a mighty fist, and feels, in relation to his family, that perhaps they had to live as they did precisely because none of them had ever done anything, right or wrong, which mattered very much. It is only he who, by an act of murder, has burst the dungeon cell. He has made it manifest that *he* lives and that his despised blood nourishes the passions of a man. He has forced his oppressors to see the fruit of that oppression: and he feels, when his family and his friends come to visit him in the death cell, that they should not be weeping or frightened, that they should be happy, *proud* that

he has dared, through murder and now through his own im-
minent destruction, to redeem their anger and humiliation,
that he has hurled into the spiritless obscurity of their lives
the lamp of his passionate life and death. Henceforth, they
may remember Bigger—who has died, as we may conclude,
for them. But they do not feel this; they only know that he
has murdered two women and precipitated a reign of terror;
and that now he is to die in the electric chair. They therefore weep and are honestly frightened—for which Bigger de-
spises them and wishes to "blot" them out. What is missing
in his situation and in the representation of his psychology—
which makes his situation false and his psychology incapable
of development—is any revelatory apprehension of Bigger
as one of the Negro's realities or as one of the Negro's roles.
This failure is part of the previously noted failure to convey
any sense of Negro life as a continuing and complex group
reality. Bigger, who cannot function therefore as a reflection
of the social illness, having, as it were, no society to reflect,
likewise refuses to function on the loftier level of the Christ-
symbol. His kinsmen are quite right to weep and be frightened, even to be appalled: for it is not his love for them or
for himself which causes him to die, but his hatred and his
self-hatred; he does not redeem the pains of a despised people, but reveals, on the contrary, nothing more than his own
fierce bitterness at having been born one of them. In this also
he is the "native son," his progress determinable by the speed
with which the distance increases between himself and the
auction-block and all that the auction-block implies. To have
penetrated this phenomenon, this inward contention of love
and hatred, blackness and whiteness, would have given him
a stature more nearly human and an end more nearly tragic;

and would have given us a document more profoundly and genuinely bitter and less harsh with an anger which is, on the one hand, exhibited and, on the other hand, denied.

Native Son finds itself at length so trapped by the American image of Negro life and by the American necessity to find the ray of hope that it cannot pursue its own implications. This is why Bigger must be at the last redeemed, to be received, if only by rhetoric, into that community of phantoms which is our tenaciously held ideal of the happy social life. It is the socially conscious whites who receive him—the Negroes being capable of no such objectivity—and we have, by way of illustration, that lamentable scene in which Jan, Mary's lover, forgives him for her murder; and, carrying the explicit burden of the novel, Max's long speech to the jury. This speech, which really ends the book, is one of the most desperate performances in American fiction. It is the question of Bigger's humanity which is at stake, the relationship in which he stands to all other Americans—and, by implication, to all people—and it is precisely this question which it cannot clarify, with which it cannot, in fact, come to any coherent terms. He is the monster created by the American republic, the present awful sum of generations of oppression; but to say that he is a monster is to fall into the trap of making him subhuman and he must, therefore, be made representative of a way of life which is real and human in precise ratio to the degree to which it seems to us monstrous and strange. It seems to me that this idea carries, implicitly, a most remarkable confession: that is, that Negro life is in fact as debased and impoverished as our theology claims; and, further, that the use to which Wright puts this idea can only proceed from the assumption—not entirely unsound—that Americans,

who evade, so far as possible, all genuine experience, have
therefore no way of assessing the experience of others and
no way of establishing themselves in relation to any way of
life which is not their own. The privacy or obscurity of Negro
life makes that life capable, in our imaginations, of producing anything at all; and thus the idea of Bigger's monstros-
ity can be presented without fear of contradiction, since no
American has the knowledge or authority to contest it and no
Negro has the voice. It is an idea, which, in the framework of
the novel, is dignified by the possibility it promptly affords of
presenting Bigger as the herald of disaster, the danger signal
of a more bitter time to come when not Bigger alone but all
his kindred will rise, in the name of the many thousands who
have perished in fire and flood and by rope and torture, to
demand their rightful vengeance.

But it is not quite fair, it seems to me, to exploit the national innocence in this way. The idea of Bigger as a warning boomerangs not only because it is quite beyond the limit
of probability that Negroes in America will ever achieve the
means of wreaking vengeance upon the state but also because it cannot be said that they have any desire to do so.
Native Son does not convey the altogether savage paradox
of the American Negro's situation, of which the social reality
which we prefer with such hopeful superficiality to study is
but, as it were, the shadow. It is not simply the relationship of
oppressed to oppressor, of master to slave, nor is it motivated
merely by hatred; it is also, literally and morally, a *blood* relationship, perhaps the most profound reality of the American
experience, and we cannot begin to unlock it until we accept
how very much it contains of the force and anguish and terror of love.

Negroes are Americans and their destiny is the country's destiny. They have no other experience besides their experience on this continent and it is an experience which cannot be rejected, which yet remains to be embraced. If, as I believe, no American Negro exists who does not have his private Bigger Thomas living in the skull, then what most significantly fails to be illuminated here is the paradoxical adjustment which is perpetually made, the Negro being compelled to accept the fact that this dark and dangerous and unloved stranger is part of himself forever. Only this recognition sets him in any wise free and it is this, this necessary ability to contain and even, in the most honorable sense of the word, to *exploit* the "nigger," which lends to Negro life its high element of the ironic and which causes the most well-meaning of their American critics to make such exhilarating errors when attempting to understand them. To present Bigger as a warning is simply to reinforce the American guilt and fear concerning him, it is most forcefully to limit him to that previously mentioned social arena in which he has no human validity, it is simply to condemn him to death. For he has always been a warning, he represents the evil, the sin and suffering which we are compelled to reject. It is useless to say to the courtroom in which this heathen sits on trial that he is their responsibility, their creation, and his crimes are theirs; and that they ought, therefore, to allow him to live, to make articulate to himself behind the walls of prison the meaning of his existence. The meaning of his existence has already been most adequately expressed, nor does anyone wish, particularly not in the name of democracy, to think of it any more; as for the possibility of articulation, it is this possibility which above all others we most dread. Moreover, the courtroom, judge, jury, witnesses and spectators, recognize immediately that Bigger is their creation and they recognize this not only with hatred and fear and guilt and the resulting fury of self-righteousness but also with that morbid fullness of pride mixed with horror with which one regards the extent and power of one's wickedness. They know that death is his portion, that he runs to death; coming from darkness and dwelling in darkness, he must be, as often as he rises, banished, lest the entire planet be engulfed. And they know, finally, that they do not wish to forgive him and that he does not wish to be forgiven; that he dies, hating them, scorning that appeal which they cannot make to that irrecoverable humanity of his which cannot hear it; and that he *wants* to die because he glories in his hatred and prefers, like Lucifer, rather to rule in hell than serve in heaven.

For, bearing in mind the premise on which the life of such a man is based, *i.e.,* that black is the color of damnation, this is his only possible end. It is the only death which will allow him a kind of dignity or even, however horribly, a kind of beauty. To tell this story, no more than a single aspect of the story of the "nigger," is inevitably and richly to become involved with the force of life and legend, how each perpetually assumes the guise of the other, creating that dense, many-sided and shifting reality which is the world we live in and the world we make. To tell his story is to begin to liberate us from his image and it is, for the first time, to clothe this phantom with flesh and blood, to deepen, by our understanding of him and his relationship to us, our understanding of ourselves and of all men.

But this is not the story which *Native Son* tells, for we find here merely, repeated in anger, the story which we have told in pride. Nor, since the implications of this anger are evaded, are we ever confronted with the actual or potential significance of our pride; which is why we fall, with such a positive glow of recognition, upon Max's long and bitter summing up. It is addressed to those among us of good will and it seems to say that, though there are whites and blacks among us who hate each other, we will not; there are those who are betrayed by greed, by guilt, by blood lust, but not we; we will set our faces against them and join hands and walk together into that dazzling future when there will be no white or black. This is the dream of all liberal men, a dream not at all dishonorable, but, nevertheless, a dream. For, let us join hands on this mountain as we may, the battle is elsewhere. It proceeds far from us in the heat and horror and pain of life itself where all men are betrayed by greed and guilt and bloodlust and where no one's hands are clean. Our good will, from which we yet expect such power to transform us, is thin, passionless, strident: its roots, examined, lead us back to our forebears, whose assumption it was that the black man, to become truly human and acceptable, must first become like us. This assumption once accepted, the Negro in America can only acquiesce in the obliteration of his own personality, the distortion and debasement of his own experience, surrendering to those forces which reduce the person to anonymity and which make themselves manifest daily all over the darkening world.

Carmen Jones: The Dark Is Light Enough

Hollywood's peculiar ability to milk, so to speak, the cow and the goat at the same time—and then to peddle the results as ginger ale—has seldom produced anything more arresting than the 1955 production of *Carmen Jones.* In Hollywood, for example, immorality and evil (which are synonyms in that lexicon) are always vividly punished, though it is the way of the transgressor—hard perhaps but far from unattractive— which keeps us on the edge of our seats, and the transgressor himself (or herself) who engages all our sympathy. Similarly, in *Carmen Jones,* the implicit parallel between an amoral Gypsy and an amoral Negro woman is the entire root idea of the show; but at the same time, bearing in mind the distances covered since *The Birth of a Nation,* it is important that the movie always be able to repudiate any suggestion that Negroes are amoral—which it can only do, considering the role of the Negro in the national psyche, by repudiating any suggestion that Negroes are not white. With a story like *Carmen* interpreted by a Negro cast this may seem a difficult assignment, but Twentieth Century-Fox has brought it off. At the same time they have also triumphantly *not* brought it

off, that is to say that the story *does* deal with amoral people,
Carmen *is* a baggage, and it *is* a Negro cast.

This is made possible in the first place, of course, by the
fact that *Carmen* is a "classic" or a "work of art" or something, therefore, sacrosanct and, luckily, quite old: it is as
ludicrously unenlightened to accuse Mérimée and Bizet
of having dirty minds as it is impossible to accuse them of
being anti-Negro. (Though it *is* possible perhaps to accuse
them of not knowing much and caring less about Gypsies.)
In the second place the music helps, for it has assuredly
never sounded so bald, or been sung so badly, or had less
relevance to life, anybody's life, than in this production. The
lyrics, too, in their way, help, being tasteless and vulgar in a
way, if not to a degree, which cannot be called characteristic
of Negroes. The movie's lifeless unreality is only occasionally
threatened by Pearl Bailey, who has, however, been fore-
stalled by Mr. Preminger's direction and is reduced—in a
series of awful costumes, designed, it would appear, to cam-
ouflage her personality—to doing what is certainly the best
that can be done with an abomination called *Beat Out That
Rhythm on a Drum* and delivering her lines for the rest of
the picture with such a murderously amused disdain that
one cannot quite avoid the suspicion that she is comment-
ing on the film. For a second or so at a time she escapes the
film's deadly inertia and in Miss Bailey one catches glimpses
of the imagination which might have exploded this movie
into something worth seeing.

But this movie, more than any movie I can remember having seen, cannot afford, dare not risk, imagination. The "sexi-
ness," for example, of Dorothy Dandridge, who plays Carmen,
becomes quite clearly manufactured and even rather silly

the moment Pearl Bailey stands anywhere near her.* And the moment one wishes that Pearl Bailey were playing Carmen one understands that *Carmen Jones* is controlled by another movie which Hollywood was studiously *not* making. For, while it is amusing to parallel Bizet's amoral Gypsy with a present-day, lower-class Negro woman, it is a good deal less amusing to parallel the Bizet violence with the violence of the Negro ghetto.

To avoid this—to exploit, that is, Carmen as a brown-skinned baggage but to avoid even suggesting any of the motivations such a present-day Carmen might have—it was helpful, first of all, that the script failed to require the services of any white people. This seals the action off, as it were, in a vacuum in which the spectacle of color is divested of its danger. The color itself then becomes a kind of vacuum which each spectator will fill with his own fantasies. But *Carmen Jones* does not inhabit the never-never land of such bogus but rather entertaining works as *Stormy Weather* or *Cabin in the Sky*—in which at least one could listen to the music; *Carmen Jones* has moved into a stratosphere rather more interesting and more pernicious, in which even Negro speech is parodied out of its charm and liberalized, if one may so put it, out of its force and precision. The result is not that the characters

---

* I have singled out Miss Bailey because the quality of her personality, forthright and wry, and with the authoritative ring of authenticity, high-lights for me the lack of any of these qualities, or any positive qualities at all, in the movie itself. She is also the only performer with whose work I am more or less familiar. Since even she is so thoroughly handicapped by the peculiar necessities of *Carmen Jones*, I should like to make it clear that, in discussing the rest of the cast, I am not trying to judge their professional competence, which, on the basis of this movie—they do not even sing in their own voices—it would be quite unfair to do.

sound like everybody else, which would be bad enough; the result is that they sound ludicrously false and affected, like ante-bellum Negroes imitating their masters. This is also the way they look, and also rather the way they are dressed, and the word that springs immediately to mind to describe the appallingly technicolored sets—an army camp, a room, and a street on Chicago's South Side, presumably, which Bigger Thomas would certainly fail to recognize—is "spotless." They could easily have been dreamed up by someone determined to prove that Negroes are as "clean" and as "modern" as white people and, I suppose, in one way or another, that is exactly how they *were* dreamed up.

And one is not allowed to forget for an instant that one is watching an opera (a word apparently synonymous in Mr. Preminger's mind with tragedy *and* fantasy), and the tone of *Carmen Jones* is stifling: a wedding of the blank, lofty solemnity with which Hollywood so often approaches "works of art" and the really quite helpless condescension with which Hollywood has always handled Negroes. The fact that one is watching a Negro cast interpreting *Carmen* is used to justify their remarkable vacuity, their complete improbability, their total divorce from anything suggestive of the realities of Negro life. On the other hand, the movie cannot possibly avoid depending very heavily on a certain quaintness, a certain lack of inhibition taken to be typical of Negroes, and further, the exigencies of the story—to say nothing of the images, which we will discuss in a moment—make it necessary to watch this movie, holding in the mind three disparate ideas: (1) that this is an opera having nothing to do with the present day, hence, nothing, *really*, to do with Negroes; but (2) the greater passion, that winning warmth (of which the movie exhibits not a trace), so typical of Negroes makes *Carmen* and ideal vehicle for their graduation into Art; and (3) these are *exceptional* Negroes, as American, that is, as you and me, interpreting lower-class Negroes of whom they, also, are very fond, an affection which is proven perhaps by the fact that everyone appears to undergo a tiny, strangling death before resolutely substituting "de" for "the."

A movie is, literally, a series of images, and what one *sees* in a movie can really be taken, beyond its stammering or misleading dialogue, as the key to what the movie is actually involved in saying. *Carmen Jones* is one of the first and most explicit—and far and away the most self-conscious— weddings of sex and color which Hollywood has yet turned out. (It will most certainly not be the last.) From this point of view the color wheel in *Carmen Jones* is very important. Dorothy Dandridge—Carmen—is a sort of taffy-colored girl, very obviously and vividly dressed, but really in herself rather more sweet than vivid. One feels—perhaps one is meant to feel—that here is a *very* nice girl making her way in movies by means of a bad-girl part; and the glow thus caused, especially since she is a colored girl, really must make up for the glow which is missing from the performance she is clearly working very hard at. Harry Belafonte is just a little darker and just as blankly handsome and fares very badly opposite her in a really offensive version of an already unendurable role. Olga James is Micaela, here called Cindy Lou, a much paler girl than Miss Dandridge but also much plainer, who is compelled to go through the entire movie in a kind of tearful stoop. Joe Adams is Husky Miller (Escamillo) and he is also rather taffy-colored, but since he is the second lead and by way of being the villain, he is not required to be as blank as

Mr. Belafonte and there is therefore, simply in his presence, some fleeting hint of masculine or at least boyish force. For the rest, Pearl Bailey is quite dark and she plays, in effect, a floozie. The wicked sergeant who causes Joe to desert the army—in one of many wildly improbable scenes—and who has evil designs on Carmen is very dark indeed; and so is Husky Miller's trainer, who is, one is given to suppose, Miss Bailey's sugar-daddy. It is quite clear that these people do not live in the same world with Carmen, or Joe, or Cindy Lou. All three of the leads are presented as indefinably complex and tragic, not after money or rhinestones but something else which causes them to be misunderstood by the more earthy types around them. This something else is love, of course, and it is with the handling of this love story that the movie really goes to town.

It is true that no one in the original *Carmen,* least of all Carmen and her lover, are very clearly motivated; but there it scarcely matters because the opera is able to get by on a purely theatrical excitement, a sort of papier-mâché violence, and the intense, if finally incredible, sexuality of its heroine. The movie does not have any of this to work with, since here excitement or violence could only blow the movie to bits, and, while the movie certainly indicates that Carmen is a luscious lollipop, it is on rather more uncertain ground when confronted with the notion of how attractive *she* finds men, and it cannot, in any case, use this as a motivating factor. Carmen is thus robbed at a stroke of even her fake vitality and all her cohesiveness and has become, instead, a nice girl, if a little fiery, whose great fault—and, since this is a tragedy, also her triumph—is that she looks at "life," as her final aria states it, "straight in de eye." In lieu of sexuality the movie-makers have dreamed up some mumbo jumbo involving buzzards' wings, signs of the zodiac, and death-dealing cards, so that, it appears, Carmen ruins Joe because she loves him and decides to leave him because the cards tell her she is going to die. The fact that between the time she leaves him and the time he kills her she acquires some new clothes, and drinks—as one of her arias rather violently indicates she intends to—a great deal of champagne is simply a sign of her intense inner suffering.

Carmen has come a long way from the auction block, but Joe, of course, cannot be far behind. This Joe is a good, fine-looking boy who loves his Maw, has studied hard, and is going to be sent to flying school, and who is engaged to a girl who rather resembles his Maw, named Cindy Lou. His indifference to Carmen, who has all the other males in sight quivering with a passion never seen on land or sea, sets her ablaze; in a series of scenes which it is difficult to call erotic without adding that they are also infantile, she goes after him and he falls. Here the technicolored bodies of Dandridge and Belafonte, while the movie is being glum about the ruin of Joe's career and impending doom, are used for the maximum erotic effect. It is a sterile and distressing eroticism, however, because it is occurring in a vacuum between two mannequins who clearly are not involved in anything more serious than giving the customers a run for their money. One is not watching either tenderness or love, and one is certainly not watching the complex and consuming passion which leads to life or death—one is watching a timorous and vulgar misrepresentation of these things.

And it must be said that one of the reasons for this is that, while the movie-makers are pleased to have Miss Dandridge

flouncing about in tight skirts and plunging necklines—
which is not exactly sexuality, either—the Negro male is still
too loaded a quantity for them to know quite how to handle.
The result is that Mr. Belafonte is really not allowed to do
anything more than walk around looking like a spaniel: *his*
sexuality is really taken as given because Miss Dandridge
wants him. It does not, otherwise, exist and he is not de-
stroyed by his own sexual aggressiveness, which he is not
allowed to have, but by the sexual aggressiveness of the
girl—or, as it turns out, not even really by that, but by tea
leaves. The only reason, finally, that the eroticism of *Carmen Jones* is more potent than, say, the eroticism of a Lana
Turner vehicle is that *Carmen Jones* has Negro bodies before the camera and Negroes are associated in the public
mind with sex. Since darker races always seem to have for
lighter races an aura of sexuality, this fact is not distressing in
itself. What is distressing is the conjecture this movie leaves
one with as to what Americans take sex to be.

The most important thing about this movie—and the
reason that, despite itself, it is one of the most important
all-Negro movies Hollywood has yet produced—is that the
questions it leaves in the mind relate less to Negroes than
to the interior life of Americans. One wonders, it is true, if
Negroes are really going to become the ciphers this movie
makes them out to be; but, since they have until now survived public images even more appalling, one is encouraged
to hope, for their sake and the sake of the Republic, that
they will continue to prove themselves incorrigible. Besides,
life does not produce ciphers like these: when people have
become this empty they are not ciphers any longer, but mon-
sters. The creation of such ciphers proves, however, that

Americans are far from empty; they are, on the contrary, very deeply disturbed. And this disturbance is not the kind which can be eased by the doing of good works, but seems to have turned inward and shows every sign of becoming personal. This is one of the best things that can possibly happen. It can be taken to mean—among a great many other things—that the ferment which has resulted in as odd a brew as *Carmen Jones* can now be expected to produce something which will be more bitter on the tongue but sweeter in the stomach.

PART TWO

The Harlem Ghetto

Harlem, physically at least, has changed very little in my parents' lifetime or in mine. Now as then the buildings are old and in desperate need of repair, the streets are crowded and dirty, there are too many human beings per square block. Rents are 10 to 58 per cent higher than anywhere else in the city; food, expensive everywhere, is more expensive here and of an inferior quality; and now that the war is over and money is dwindling, clothes are carefully shopped for and seldom bought. Negroes, traditionally the last to be hired and the first to be fired, are finding jobs harder to get, and, while prices are rising implacably, wages are going down. All over Harlem now there is felt the same bitter expectancy with which, in my childhood, we awaited winter: it is coming and it will be hard; there is nothing anyone can do about it.

All of Harlem is pervaded by a sense of congestion, rather like the insistent, maddening, claustrophobic pounding in the skull that comes from trying to breathe in a very small room with all the windows shut. Yet the white man walking through Harlem is not at all likely to find it sinister or more wretched than any other slum.

Harlem wears to the casual observer a casual face; no one remarks that—considering the history of black men and women and the legends that have sprung up about them, to say nothing of the ever-present policemen, wary on the street corners—the face is, indeed, somewhat excessively casual and may not be as open or as careless as it seems. If an outbreak of more than usual violence occurs, as in 1935 or in 1943, it is met with sorrow and surprise and rage; the social hostility of the rest of the city feeds on this as proof that they were right all along, and the hostility increases; speeches are made, committees are set up, investigations ensue. Steps are taken to right the wrong, without, however, expanding or demolishing the ghetto. The idea is to make it less of a social liability, a process about as helpful as make-up to a leper. Thus, we have the Boys' Club on West 134th Street, the playground at West 131st and Fifth Avenue; and, since Negroes will not be allowed to live in Stuyvesant Town, Metropolitan Life is thoughtfully erecting a housing project called Riverton in the center of Harlem; however, it is not likely that any but the professional class of Negroes—and not all of them—will be able to pay the rent.

Most of these projects have been stimulated by perpetually embattled Negro leaders and by the Negro press. Concerning Negro leaders, the best that one can say is that they are in an impossible position and that the handful motivated by genuine concern maintain this position with heartbreaking dignity. It is unlikely that anyone acquainted with Harlem seriously assumes that the presence of one playground more or less has any profound effect upon the psychology of the citizens there. And yet it is better to have the playground; it is better than nothing; and it will, at least, make life somewhat easier for parents who will then know that their children are not in as much danger of being run down in the streets. Similarly, even though the American cult of literacy has chiefly operated only to provide a market for the *Reader's Digest* and the *Daily News,* literacy is still better than illiteracy; so Negro leaders must demand more and better schools for Negroes, though any Negro who takes this schooling at face value will find himself virtually incapacitated for life in this democracy. Possibly the most salutary effect of all this activity is that it assures the Negro that he is not altogether forgotten: people *are* working in his behalf, however hopeless or misguided they may be; and as long as the water is troubled it cannot become stagnant.

The terrible thing about being a Negro leader lies in the term itself. I do not mean merely the somewhat condescending differentiation the term implies, but the nicely refined torture a man can experience from having been created and defeated by the same circumstances. That is, Negro leaders have been created by the American scene, which thereafter works against them at every point; and the best that they can hope for is ultimately to work themselves out of their jobs, to nag contemporary American leaders and the members of their own group until a bad situation becomes so complicated and so bad that it cannot be endured any longer. It is like needling a blister until it bursts. On the other hand, one cannot help observing that some Negro leaders and politicians are far more concerned with their careers than with the welfare of Negroes, and their dramatic and publicized battles are battles with the wind. Again, this phenomenon cannot be changed without a change in the American scene. In a land where, it is said, any citizen can grow up and become president, Negroes can be pardoned for desiring to enter Congress.

The Negro press, which supports any man, provided he is sufficiently dark and well-known—with the exception of certain Negro novelists accused of drawing portraits unflattering to the race—has for years received vastly confusing criticism based on the fact that it is helplessly and always exactly what it calls itself, that is, a press devoted entirely to happenings in or about the Negro world. This preoccupation can probably be forgiven in view of the great indifference and frequent hostility of the American white press. The Negro press has been accused of not helping matters much—as indeed, it has not, nor do I see how it could have. And it has been accused of being sensational, which it is; but this is a criticism difficult to take seriously in a country so devoted to the sensational as ours.

The best-selling Negro newspaper, I believe, is the *Amsterdam Star-News,* which is also the worst, being gleefully devoted to murders, rapes, raids on love-nests, interracial wars, any item—however meaningless—concerning prominent Negroes, and whatever racial gains can be reported for the week—all in just about that order. Apparently, this policy works well; it sells papers—which is, after all, the aim; in my childhood we never missed an edition. The day the paper came out we could hear, far down the street, the news vendor screaming the latest scandal and people rushing to read about it.

The *Amsterdam* has been rivaled, in recent years, by the *People's Voice,* a journal, modeled on *PM* and referred to as *PV. PV* is not so wildly sensational a paper as the *Amsterdam,* though its coverage is much the same (the news coverage of the Negro press is naturally pretty limited). *PV*'s politics are less murky, to the left of center (the *Amsterdam* is Republican, a political affiliation that has led it into some strange doubletalk), and its tone, since its inception, has been ever more hopelessly militant, full of warnings, appeals, and open letters to the government—which, to no one's surprise, are not answered—and the same rather pathetic preoccupation with prominent Negroes and what they are doing. Columns signed by Lena Horne and Paul Robeson appeared in *PV* until several weeks ago, when both severed their connections with the paper. Miss Horne's column made her sound like an embittered Eleanor Roosevelt, and the only column of Robeson's I have read was concerned with the current witch-hunt in Hollywood, discussing the kind of movies under attack and Hollywood's traditional treatment of Negroes. It is personally painful to me to realize that so gifted and forceful a man as Robeson should have been tricked by his own bitterness and by a total inability to understand the nature of political power in general, or Communist aims in particular, into missing the point of his own critique, which is worth a great deal of thought: that there are a great many ways of being un-American, some of them nearly as old as the country itself, and that the House Un-American Activities Committee might find concepts and attitudes even more damaging to American life in a picture like *Gone With the Wind* than in the possibly equally romantic but far less successful *Watch on the Rhine.*

The only other newspapers in the field with any significant sale in Harlem are the Pittsburgh *Courier,* which has the reputation of being the best of the lot, and the *Afro-American,* which resembles the New York *Journal-American* in layout and type and seems to make a consistent if unsuccessful effort to be at once readable, intelligent, and fiery. The *Courier* is a high-class paper, reaching its peak in the handling of its society news and in the columns of George S. Schuyler, whose Olympian serenity infuriates me, but who, as a matter of fact, reflects with great accuracy the state of mind and the ambitions of the professional, well-to-do Negro who has managed to find a place to stand. Mr. Schuyler, who is remembered still for a satirical novel I have not read, called *Black No More,* is aided enormously in this position by a genteel white wife and a child-prodigy daughter—who is seriously regarded in some circles as proof of the incomprehensible contention that the mating of white and black is more likely to produce genius than any other combination. (The *Afro-American* recently ran a series of articles on this subject, "The Education of a Genius," by Mrs. Amarintha Work, who recorded in detail the development of her mulatto son, Craig.)

Ebony and *Our World* are the two big magazines in the field, *Ebony* looking and sounding very much like *Life,* and *Our World* being the black man's *Look. Our World* is a very strange, disorganized magazine indeed, sounding sometimes like a college newspaper and sometimes like a call to arms, but principally, like its more skillful brothers, devoted to the proposition that anything a white man can do a Negro can probably do better. *Ebony* digs feature articles out of such things as the "real" Lena Horne and Negro FBI agents, and it travels into the far corners of the earth for any news, however trivial, concerning any Negro or group of Negroes who are in any way unusual and/or newsworthy. The tone of both *Ebony* and *Our World* is affirmative; they cater to the "better class of Negro." *Ebony's* November 1947 issue carried an editoral entitled "Time To Count Our Blessings," which began by accusing Chester Himes (author of the novel *Lonely Crusade*) of having a color psychosis, and went on to explain that there are Negro racists also who are just as blind and dangerous as Bilbo, which is incontestably true, and that, compared to the millions of starving Europeans, Negroes are sitting pretty—which comparison, I hazard, cannot possibly mean anything to any Negro who has not seen Europe. The editorial concluded that Negroes had come a long way and that "as patriotic Americans" it was time "we" stopped singing the blues and realized just how bright the future was. These cheering sentiments were flanked—or underscored, if you will—by a photograph on the opposite page of an aging Negro farm woman carrying home a bumper crop of onions. It apparently escaped the editors of *Ebony* that the very existence of their magazine, and its table of contents for any month, gave the lie to this effort to make the best of a bad bargain.

The true *raison d'être* of the Negro press can be found in the letters-to-the-editor sections, where the truth about life among the rejected can be seen in print. It is the terrible dilemma of the Negro press that, having no other model, it models itself on the white press, attempting to emulate the same effortless, sophisticated tone—a tone its subject matter renders utterly unconvincing. It is simply impossible not to sing the blues, audibly or not, when the lives lived by Negroes are so inescapably harsh and stunted. It is not the Negro press that is at fault: whatever contradictions, inanities, and political infantilism can be charged to it can be charged equally to the American press at large. It is a black man's newspaper straining for recognition and a foothold in the white man's world. Matters are not helped in the least by the fact that the white man's world, intellectually, morally, and spiritually, has the meaningless ring of a hollow drum and the odor of slow death. Within the body of the Negro press all the wars and falsehoods, all the decay and dislocation and struggle of our society are seen in relief.

The Negro press, like the Negro, becomes the scapegoat for our ills. There is no difference, after all, between the *Amsterdam's* handling of a murder on Lenox Avenue and the *Daily News'* coverage of a murder on Beekman Hill; nor is there any difference between the chauvinism of the two papers, except that the *News* is smug and the *Amsterdam* is desperate. Negroes live violent lives, unavoidably; a Negro press without violence is therefore not possible; and, further, in every act of violence, particularly violence against white men, Negroes feel a certain thrill of identification, a wish to have done it themselves, a feeling that old scores are being settled at last. It is no accident that Joe Louis is the most idolized man in Harlem. He has succeeded on a level that white America indicates is the only level for which it has any respect. We (Americans in general, that is) like to point to Negroes and to most of their activities with a kind of tolerant scorn; but it is ourselves we are watching, ourselves we are damning, or—condescendingly—bending to save.

I have written at perhaps excessive length about the Negro press, principally because its many critics have always seemed to me to make the irrational demand that the nation's most oppressed minority behave itself at all times with a skill and foresight no one ever expected of the late Joseph Patterson or ever expected of Hearst; and I have tried to give some idea of its tone because it seems to me that it is here that the innate desperation is betrayed. As for the question of Negro advertising, which has caused so much comment, it seems to me quite logical that any minority identified by the color of its skin and the texture of its hair would eventually grow self-conscious about these attributes and avoid advertising lotions that made the hair kinkier and soaps that darkened the skin. The American ideal, after all, is that everyone should be as much alike as possible.

It is axiomatic that the Negro is religious, which is to say that he stands in fear of the God our ancestors gave us and before whom we all tremble yet. There are probably more churches in Harlem than in any other ghetto in this city and they are going full blast every night and some of them are filled with praying people every day. This, supposedly, exemplifies the Negro's essential simplicity and good-will; but it is actually a fairly desperate emotional business.

These churches range from the august and publicized Abyssinian Baptist Church on West 138th Street to resolutely unclassifiable lofts, basements, store-fronts, and even private dwellings. Nightly, Holyroller ministers, spiritualists, self-appointed prophets and Messiahs gather their flocks together for worship and for strength through joy. And this is not, as *Cabin in the Sky* would have us believe, merely a childlike emotional release. Their faith may be described as childlike, but the end it serves is often sinister. It may, indeed, "keep them happy"—a phrase carrying the inescapable inference that the way of life imposed on Negroes makes them quite actively unhappy—but also, and much more significantly, religion operates here as a complete and exquisite fantasy revenge: white people own the earth and commit all manner of abomination and injustice on it; the bad will be punished and the good rewarded, for God is not sleeping, the judgment is not far off. It does not require a spectacular degree of perception to realize that bitterness is here neither dead nor sleeping, and that the white man, believing what he wishes to believe, has misread the symbols. Quite often the Negro preacher descends to levels less abstract and leaves no doubt as to what is on his mind: the pressure of life in Harlem, the conduct of the Italian-Ethiopian war, racial injustice during the recent war, and the terrible possibility of yet another very soon. All these topics provide excellent springboards for sermons thinly coated with spirituality but designed mainly to illustrate the injustice of the white American and anticipate his certain and long overdue punishment.

Here, too, can be seen one aspect of the Negro's ambivalent relation to the Jew. To begin with, though the traditional Christian accusation that the Jews killed Christ is neither questioned nor doubted, the term "Jew" actually operates in this initial context to include all infidels of white skin who have failed to accept the Savior. No real distinction is made: the preacher begins by accusing the Jews of having refused the light and proceeds from there to a catalog of their subsequent sins and the sufferings visited on them by a wrathful God. Though the notion of the suffering is based on the image of the wandering, exiled Jew, the context changes imperceptibly, to become a fairly obvious reminder of the trials of the Negro, while the sins recounted are the sins of the American republic.

At this point, the Negro identifies himself almost wholly with the Jew. The more devout Negro considers that he *is* a Jew, in bondage to a hard taskmaster and waiting for a Moses to lead him out of Egypt. The hymns, the texts, and the most favored legends of the devout Negro are all Old Testament and therefore Jewish in origin: the flight from Egypt, the Hebrew children in the fiery furnace, the terrible jubilee songs

of deliverance: *Lord, wasn't that hard trials, great tribula-
tions, I'm bound to leave this land!* The covenant God made
in the beginning with Abraham and which was to extend to his
children and to his children's children forever is a covenant
made with these latter-day exiles also: as Israel was chosen,
so are they. The birth and death of Jesus, which adds a non-
Judaic element, also implements this identification. It is the
covenant made with Abraham again, renewed, signed with his
blood. ("Before Abraham was, I am.") Here the figure of Jesus
operates as the intercessor, the bridge from earth to heaven;
it was Jesus who made it possible, who made salvation free to
all, "to the Jew first and afterwards the Gentile." The images
of the suffering Christ and the suffering Jew are wedded with
the image of the suffering slave, and they are one: the people
that walked in darkness have seen a great light.

But if the Negro has bought his salvation with pain and
the New Testament is used to prove, as it were, the validity of the transformation, it is the Old Testament which is
clung to and most frequently preached from, which provides
the emotional fire and anatomizes the path of bondage; and
which promises vengeance and assures the chosen of their
place in Zion. The favorite text of my father, among the most
earnest of ministers, was not "Father, forgive them, for they
know not what they do," but "How can I sing the Lord's song
in a strange land?"

This same identification, which Negroes, since slavery,
have accepted with their mothers' milk, serves, in contemporary actuality, to implement an involved and specific bitterness. Jews in Harlem are small tradesmen, rent collectors,
real estate agents, and pawnbrokers; they operate in accor-
dance with the American business tradition of exploiting

Negroes, and they are therefore identified with oppression and are hated for it. I remember meeting no Negro in the years of my growing up, in my family or out of it, who would really ever trust a Jew, and few who did not, indeed, exhibit for them the blackest contempt. On the other hand, this did not prevent their working for Jews, being utterly civil and pleasant to them, and, in most cases, contriving to delude their employers into believing that, far from harboring any dislike for Jews, they would rather work for a Jew than for anyone else. It is part of the price the Negro pays for his position in this society that, as Richard Wright points out, he is almost always acting. A Negro learns to gauge precisely what reaction the alien person facing him desires, and he produces it with disarming artlessness. The friends I had, growing up and going to work, grew more bitter every day; and, conversely, they learned to hide this bitterness and to fit into the pattern Gentile and Jew alike had fixed for them.

The tension between Negroes and Jews contains an element not characteristic of Negro-Gentile tension, an element which accounts in some measure for the Negro's tendency to castigate the Jew verbally more often than the Gentile, and which might lead one to the conclusion that, of all white people on the face of the earth, it is the Jew whom the Negro hates most. When the Negro hates the Jew *as a Jew* he does so partly because the nation does and in much the same painful fashion that he hates himself. It is an aspect of his humiliation whittled down to a manageable size and then transferred; it is the best form the Negro has for tabulating vocally his long record of grievances against his native land.

At the same time, there is a subterranean assumption that the Jew should "know better," that he has suffered enough himself to know what suffering means. An understanding is expected of the Jew such as none but the most naïve and visionary Negro has ever expected of the American Gentile. The Jew, by the nature of his own precarious position, has failed to vindicate this faith. Jews, like Negroes, must use every possible weapon in order to be accepted, and must try to cover their vulnerability by a frenzied adoption of the customs of the country; and the nation's treatment of Negroes is unquestionably a custom. The Jew has been taught—and, too often, accepts—the legend of Negro inferiority; and the Negro, on the other hand, has found nothing in his experience with Jews to counteract the legend of Semitic greed. Here the American white Gentile has two legends serving him at once: he has divided these minorities and he rules.

It seems unlikely that within this complicated structure any real and systematic cooperation can be achieved between Negroes and Jews. (This is in terms of the over-all social problem and is not meant to imply that individual friendships are impossible or that they are valueless when they occur.) The structure of the American commonwealth has trapped both these minorities into attitudes of perpetual hostility. They do not dare trust each other—the Jew because he feels he must climb higher on the American social ladder and has, so far as he is concerned, nothing to gain from identification with any minority even more unloved than he; while the Negro is in the even less tenable position of not really daring to trust anyone.

This applies, with qualifications and yet with almost no exceptions, even to those Negroes called progressive and "unusual." Negroes of the professional class (as distinct from professional Negroes) compete actively with the Jew in daily

contact; and they wear anti-Semitism as a defiant proof of
their citizenship; their positions are too shaky to allow them
any real ease or any faith in anyone. They do not trust whites
or each other or themselves; and, particularly and vocally,
they do not trust Jews. During my brief days as a Socialist I
spent more than one meeting arguing against anti-Semitism
with a Negro college student, who was trying to get into civil
service and was supporting herself meanwhile as a domestic.
She was by no means a stupid girl, nor even a particularly
narrow-minded one: she was all in favor of the millennium,
even to working with Jews to achieve it; but she was not prepared ever to accept a Jew as a friend. It did no good to point
out, as I did, that the exploitation of which she accused the
Jews was American, not Jewish, that in fact, behind the Jewish face stood the American reality. And *my* Jewish friends in
high school were not like that, I said, they had no intention
of exploiting *me,* we did not hate each other. (I remember, as
I spoke, being aware of doubt crawling like fog in the back of
my mind.) This might all be very well, she told me, we were
children now, with no need to earn a living. Wait until later,
when your friends go into business and you try to get a job.
You'll see!

It is this bitterness—felt alike by the inarticulate, hungry
population of Harlem, by the wealthy on Sugar Hill, and by
the brilliant exceptions ensconced in universities—which
has defeated and promises to continue to defeat all efforts
at interracial understanding. I am not one of the people who
believe that oppression imbues a people with wisdom or in-
sight or sweet charity, though the survival of the Negro in
this country would simply not have been possible if this bitterness had been all he felt. In America, though, life seems to

move faster than anywhere else on the globe and each generation is promised more than it will get: which creates, in each generation, a furious, bewildered rage, the rage of people who cannot find solid ground beneath their feet. Just as a mountain of sociological investigations, committee reports, and plans for recreational centers have failed to change the face of Harlem or prevent Negro boys and girls from growing up and facing, individually and alone, the unendurable frustration of being always, everywhere, inferior—until finally the cancer attacks the mind and warps it—so there seems no hope for better Negro-Jewish relations without a change in the American pattern.

Both the Negro and the Jew are helpless; the pressure of living is too immediate and incessant to allow time for understanding. I can conceive of no Negro native to this country who has not, by the age of puberty, been irreparably scarred by the conditions of his life. All over Harlem, Negro boys and girls are growing into stunted maturity, trying desperately to find a place to stand; and the wonder is not that so many are ruined but that so many survive. The Negro's outlets are desperately constricted. In his dilemma he turns first upon himself and then upon whatever most represents to him his own emasculation. Here the Jew is caught in the American crossfire. The Negro, facing a Jew, hates, at bottom, not his Jewishness but the color of his skin. It is not the Jewish tradition by which he has been betrayed but the tradition of his native land. But just as a society must have a scapegoat, so hatred must have a symbol. Georgia has the Negro and Harlem has the Jew.

Journey to Atlanta

The Progressive Party has not, so far as I can gather, made any very great impression in Harlem, and this is not so much despite as because of its campaign promises, promises rather too extravagant to be believed. It is considered a rather cheerful axiom that all Americans distrust politicians. (No one takes the further and less cheerful step of considering just what effect this mutual contempt has on either the public or the politicians, who have, indeed, very little to do with one another.) Of all Americans, Negroes distrust politicians most, or, more accurately, they have been best trained to expect nothing from them; more than other Americans, they are always aware of the enormous gap between election promises and their daily lives. It is true that the promises excite them, but this is not because they are taken as proof of good intentions. They are the proof of something more concrete than intentions: that the Negro situation is not static, that changes have occurred, and are occurring and will occur—this, in spite of the daily, dead-end monotony. It is this daily, dead-end monotony, though, as well as the wise desire not to be betrayed by too much hoping, which causes them to look on politicians with such an extraordinarily disenchanted eye.

This fatalistic indifference is something that drives the optimistic American liberal quite mad; he is prone, in his more
exasperated moments, to refer to Negroes as political children, an appellation not entirely just. Negro liberals, being
consulted, assure us that this is something that will disappear with "education," a vast, all-purpose term, conjuring up
visions of sunlit housing projects, stacks of copybooks and
a race of well-soaped, dark-skinned people who never slur
their R's. Actually, this is not so much political irresponsibility as the product of experience, experience which no
amount of education can quite efface. It is, as much as anything else, the reason the Negro vote is so easily bought and
sold, the reason for that exclamation heard so frequently on
Sugar Hill: "Our people never get anywhere."

"Our people" have functioned in this country for nearly
a century as political weapons, the trump card up the enemies' sleeve; anything promised Negroes at election time
is also a threat levelled at the opposition; in the struggle for
mastery the Negro is the pawn. It is inescapable that this is
only possible because of his position in this country and it has
very frequently seemed at least equally apparent that this is
a position which no one, least of all the politician, seriously
intended to change.

Since Negroes have been in this country their one major,
devastating gain was their Emancipation, an emancipation
no one regards any more as having been dictated by hu-
manitarian impulses. All that has followed from that brings
to mind the rather unfortunate image of bones thrown to a
pack of dogs sufficiently hungry to be dangerous. If all this
sounds rather deliberately grim, it is not through any wish
to make the picture darker than it is; I would merely like to

complete the picture usually presented by pointing out that no matter how many instances there have been of genuine concern and good-will, nor how many hard, honest struggles have been carried on to improve the position of the Negro people, their position has not, in fact, changed so far as most of them are concerned.

Sociologists and historians, having the historical perspective in mind, may conclude that we are moving toward ever-greater democracy; but this is beyond the ken of a Negro growing up in any one of this country's ghettos. As regards Negro politicians, they are considered with pride as *politicians,* a pride much akin to that felt concerning Marian Anderson or Joe Louis: they have proven the worth of the Negro people and in terms, American terms, which no one can negate. But as no housewife expects Marian Anderson's genius to be of any practical aid in her dealings with the landlord, so nothing is expected of Negro representatives. The terrible thing, and here we have an American phenomenon in relief, is the fact that the Negro representative, by virtue of his position, is ever more removed from the people he ostensibly serves. Moreover, irrespective of personal integrity, his position—neatly and often painfully paradoxical—is utterly dependent on the continuing debasement of fourteen million Negroes; should the national ideals be put into practice tomorrow, countless prominent Negroes would lose their *raison d'être.*

Finally, we are confronted with the psychology and tradition of the country; if the Negro vote is so easily bought and sold, it is because it has been treated with so little respect; since no Negro dares seriously assume that any politician is concerned with the fate of Negroes, or would do much about it if he had the power, the vote must be bartered for what it will get, for whatever short-term goals can be managed. These goals are mainly economic and frequently personal, sometimes pathetic: bread or a new roof or five dollars, or, continuing up the scale, schools, houses or more Negroes in hitherto Caucasian jobs. The American commonwealth chooses to overlook what Negroes are never able to forget: they are not *really* considered a part of it. Like Aziz in *A Passage to India* or Topsy in *Uncle Tom's Cabin,* they know that white people, whatever their love for justice, have no love for them.

This is the crux of the matter; and the Progressive Party, with its extravagant claims, has, therefore, imposed on itself the considerable burden of proof. The only party within recent memory which made equally strident claims of fellowship were the Communists, who failed to survive this test; and the only politician of similar claims was, of course, Wallace's erstwhile master, Roosevelt, who did not after all, now that the magic of his voice is gone, succeed in raising the darker brother to the status of a citizen. This is the ancestry of the Wallace party, and it does not work wholly in its favor. It operates to give pause to even the most desperate and the most gullible.

It is, however, considered on one level, the level of short-term goals, with approval, since it does afford temporary work for Negroes, particularly those associated in any manner with the arts. The rather flippant question on 125th Street now is: "So? You working for Mr. Wallace these days?" For at least there is that: entertainers, personalities are in demand. To forestall lawsuits, I must explain that I am not discussing "names"—who are in rather a different position, too touchy and complex to analyze here—but the unknown, the struggling, endless armies of Negro boys and girls bent on, and as yet very far from, recognition. A segment of this army, a quartet called *The Melodeers,* made a trip to Atlanta under the auspices of the Progressive Party in August, a trip which lasted about eighteen days and which left them with no love for Mr. Wallace. Since this quartet included two of my brothers, I was given the details of the trip; indeed, David, the younger, kept a sort of journal for me—literally a blow-by-blow account.

Harlem is filled with churches and on Sundays it gives the impression of being filled with music. Quartets such as my brothers' travel from church to church in the fashion of circuit preachers, singing as much for the love of singing and the need for practice as for the rather indifferent sums collected for them which are then divided. These quartets have "battles of song," the winning team adding, of course, immensely to its prestige, the most consistent winners being the giants in this field. The aim of all these quartets, of course, is to branch out, to hit the big time and sing for a livelihood. The Golden Gate Quartet, judging at least from its music, had its roots here, and out of such a background came Sister Rosetta Tharpe, whom I heard, not quite ten years ago, plunking a guitar in a storefront church on Fifth Avenue. *The Melodeers* have not been singing very long and are very far from well-known, and the invitation to sing on tour with the Wallace party in the South seemed, whatever their misgivings about the Mason-Dixon line, too good an opportunity to pass up.

This invitation, by the way, seems to have been the brain-storm of a Clarence Warde, a Negro merchant seaman once employed as a cottage father in a corrective institution upstate; it was he in New York who acted as a go-between,

arranging, since *The Melodeers* are minors, to be their legal
guardian and manager on the road. An extended tour, such
as was planned, met with some opposition from the parents,
an opposition countered by the possible long-term benefits
of the tour in so far as the boys' careers were concerned and,
even more urgently, by the assurance that, at the very least,
the boys would come home with a considerably larger sum of
money than any of them were making on their jobs. (The political implications do not seem to have carried much weight.)
A series of churches had been lined up for them presumably
throughout the South. "The understanding," writes David,
"was that we were supposed to sing"; after which the party
was to take over to make speeches and circulate petitions.
"The arrangement," David notes laconically, "sounded very
promising, so we decided to go."

And, indeed, they traveled South in splendor, in a Pullman, to be exact, in which, since what David describes as a
"Southern gentleman and wife" took exception to their presence, they traveled alone.

At the Wallace headquarters in Atlanta they were introduced
to a Mrs. Branson Price, a grey-haired white woman of in-
curably aristocratic leanings who seems to have been the di-
rectress of the party in that region. The graciousness of her
reception was only slightly marred by the fact that she was
not expecting singers and thought they were a new group of
canvassers. She arranged for them to take rooms on Butler
Street at the YMCA. Here the first gap between promise and
performance was made manifest, a gap, they felt, which was
perhaps too trifling to make a fuss about. In New York they

had been promised comparative privacy, two to a room; but now, it developed, they were to sleep in a dormitory. This gap, in fact, it was the province of Mr. Warde to close, but whether he was simply weary from the trip or overwhelmed by the aristocratic Mrs. Price, he kept his mouth shut and, indeed, did not open it again for quite some time.

When they returned to headquarters, somewhat irritated at having had to wait three hours for the arrival of Louis Burner, who had the money for their rooms, Mrs. Price suggested that they go out canvassing. This was wholly unexpected, since no one had mentioned canvassing in New York and, since, moreover, canvassers are voluntary workers who are not paid. Further, the oldest of them was twenty, which was not voting age, and none of them knew anything about the Progressive Party, nor did they care much. On the other hand, it is somewhat difficult to refuse a grey-haired, aristocratic lady who is toiling day and night for the benefit of your people; and Mr. Warde, who should have been their spokesman, had not yet recovered his voice; so they took the petitions, which were meant to put the Wallace party on the ballot, and began knocking on doors in the Negro section of Atlanta. They were sent out in pairs, white and black, a political device which operates not only as the living proof of brotherhood, but which has the additional virtue of intimidating into passive silence the more susceptible beholder, who cannot, after all, unleash the impatient scorn he may feel with a strange, benevolent white man sitting in his parlor.

They canvassed for three days, during which time their expenses—$2.25 per man per day—were paid, but during which time they were doing no singing and making no money. On the third day they pointed out that this was not quite what they had been promised in New York, to be met with another suggestion from the invincible Mrs. Price: how would they like to sing on the sound-truck? They had not the faintest desire to sing on a sound-truck, especially when they had been promised a string of churches; however, the churches, along with Mr. Warde's vigor, seemed unavailable at the moment; they could hardly sit around Atlanta doing nothing; and so long as they worked with the party they were certain, at least, to be fed. "The purpose of our singing," David writes, "was to draw a crowd so the party could make speeches." Near the end of the singing and during the speeches, leaflets and petitions were circulated through the crowd.

David had not found Negroes in the South different in any important respect from Negroes in the North; except that many of them were distrustful and "they are always talking about the North; they have to let you know they know somebody in New York or Chicago or Detroit." Of the crowds that gathered—and, apparently, *The Melodeers* attracted great numbers—"many of these people couldn't read or write their names" and not many of them knew anything at all about the Progressive Party. But they did divine, as American Negroes must, what was expected of them; and they listened to the speeches and signed the petitions.

Becoming both desperate and impatient, *The Melodeers* began making engagements and singing on their own, stealing time from canvassing to rehearse. They made more appointments than they were able to keep; partly because the lack of money limited their mobility but also because the Party, discovering these clandestine appointments, moved in, demanding to be heard. Those churches which refused to make room for the Party were not allowed to hear the quartet, which thus lost its last hope of making any money. The quartet wondered what had happened to Mr. Warde. David's account all but ignores him until nearly the end of the trip, when his position during all this is perhaps given some illumination.

Things now began to go steadily worse. They got into an argument with the manager of the Y, who objected to their rehearsing, and moved to a private home, for which the Party paid 75¢ per man per day; and the Party, which was, one gathers, furiously retrenching, arranged for them to eat at Fraziers' Cafe, a Negro establishment on Hunter Street, for $1.25 per man per day. My correspondent notes that they had no choice of meals—"they served us what they liked"— which seems to have been mainly limp vegetables—and "we were as hungry when we walked out as we were when we walked in." On the other hand, they were allowed to choose their beverage: tea or coffee or soda pop.

Heaven only knows what prompted Mrs. Branson Price to give a party at this point. Perhaps the campaign was going extraordinarily well; perhaps Fraziers' Cafe, where the party was held, was in need of a little extra revenue as well as the knowledge that its adoption of the Party would help to bring about a better world; perhaps Mrs. Price merely longed to be a gracious hostess once again. In any case, on a Sunday night she gave a party to which everyone was invited. My brother, who at this point was much concerned with food, observed glumly, "We had ice-cream."

The quartet sat at a table by itself, robbed, however, of the presence of Mr. Warde, who was invited to sit at Mrs. Price's table: "she said it would be an honor," my correspondent notes, failing, however, to say for whom. "There was a man there called a *folk*-singer," says David with venom, "and, naturally, everybody had to hear some *folk* songs." Eventually, the folksy aspect of the evening was exhausted and the quartet was invited to sing. They sang four selections, apparently to everyone's delight for they had to be quite adamant about not singing a fifth. The strain of continual singing in the open air had done their voices no good and it had made one of them extremely hoarse. So they refused, over loud protests, and apologized. "This displeased Mrs. Price."

Indeed, it had. She was not in the least accustomed to having her suggestions, to say nothing of her requests, refused. Early Monday morning she called Mr. Warde to her office to inquire who those black boys thought they were? and determined to ship them all back that same day in a car. Mr. Warde, who, considering the honors of the evening before, must have been rather astounded, protested such treatment, to be warned that she might very well ship them off without a car; the six of them might very well be forced to take to the road. This is not a pleasant mode of traveling for a Negro in the North and no Negro in Atlanta, particularly no Northern Negro, is likely to get very far. Mr. Warde temporized: they could not leave on such short notice; for one thing, the boys had clothes at the cleaners which would not be ready for a while and which they could hardly afford to lose. Mrs. Price, every aristocratic vein pounding, did not wish to be concerned with such plebeian matters and, finally, losing all patience, commanded Mr. Warde to leave her office: Had he forgotten that he was in Georgia? Didn't he know better than sit in a white woman's office?

Mr. Warde, in whose bowels last night's bread of fellowship must have acquired the weight of rock, left the office. Then the quartet attempted to secure an audience; to be met with implacable refusal and the threat of the police. There were, incidentally, according to my brother, five Negro policemen in Atlanta at this time, who, though they were not allowed to arrest whites, would, of course, be willing, indeed, in their position, anxious, to arrest any Negro who seemed to need it. In Harlem, Negro policemen are feared even more than whites, for they have more to prove and fewer ways to prove it. The prospect of being arrested in Atlanta made them a little dizzy with terror: what might mean a beating in Harlem might quite possibly mean death here. "And at the same time," David says, "it was funny"; by which he means that the five policemen were faint prophecies of that equality which is the Progressive Party's goal.

They did not see Mrs. Price again; this was their severance from the Party, which now refused to pay any expenses; it was only the fact that their rent had been paid in advance which kept them off the streets. Food, however, remained a problem. Mr. Warde brought them a "couple of loaves of bread" and some jam; they sang one engagement. During this week Mrs. Price relented enough to get their clothes from the cleaners and send Mr. Warde, in custody of a white man who had been at the party, to the bus station for tickets. This man, whose resemblance to the Southern Gentleman of the Pullman is in no way diminished by his allegiance to Mr. Wallace, bought the tickets and threw them on the ground at Mr. Warde's feet, advising him not to show his black face in Georgia again.

The quartet, meanwhile, had gotten together six dollars doing odd jobs, which was enough, perhaps, for three of them to eat on the road. They split up, three leaving that Friday and the other two staying on about ten days longer, working for a construction company. Mr. Warde stopped off to visit his family, promising to see *The Melodeers* in New York, but he had not arrived as this was being written. *Then Melodeers* laugh about their trip now, that good-natured, hearty laughter which is, according to white men, the peculiar heritage of Negroes, Negroes who were born with the fortunate ability to laugh all their troubles away. Somewhat surprisingly, they are not particularly bitter toward the Progressive Party, though they can scarcely be numbered among its supporters. "They're all the same," David tells me, "ain't none of 'em gonna do you no good; if you gonna be foolish enough to believe what they say, then it serves you good and right. Ain't none of 'em gonna do a thing for *me*."

Notes of a Native Son

On the 29th of July, in 1943, my father died. On the same day, a few hours later, his last child was born. Over a month before this, while all our energies were concentrated in waiting for these events, there had been, in Detroit, one of the bloodiest race riots of the century. A few hours after my father's funeral, while he lay in state in the undertaker's chapel, a race riot broke out in Harlem. On the morning of the 3rd of August, we drove my father to the graveyard through a wilderness of smashed plate glass.

The day of my father's funeral had also been my nineteenth birthday. As we drove him to the graveyard, the spoils of injustice, anarchy, discontent, and hatred were all around us. It seemed to me that God himself had devised, to mark my father's end, the most sustained and brutally dissonant of codas. And it seemed to me, too, that the violence which rose all about us as my father left the world had been devised as a corrective for the pride of his eldest son. I had declined to believe in that apocalypse which had been central to my father's vision; very well, life seemed to be saying, here is something that will certainly pass for an apocalypse until the real thing comes along. I had inclined to be contemptuous of my father for the conditions of his life, for the conditions of our lives. When his life had ended I began to wonder about that life and also, in a new way, to be apprehensive about my own.

I had not known my father very well. We had got on badly, partly because we shared, in our different fashions, the vice of stubborn pride. When he was dead I realized that I had hardly ever spoken to him. When he had been dead a long time I began to wish I had. It seems to be typical of life in America, where opportunities, real and fancied, are thicker than anywhere else on the globe, that the second generation has no time to talk to the first. No one, including my father, seems to have known exactly how old he was, but his mother had been born during slavery. He was of the first generation of free men. He, along with thousands of other Negroes, came North after 1919 and I was part of that generation which had never seen the landscape of what Negroes sometimes call the Old Country.

He had been born in New Orleans and had been a quite young man there during the time that Louis Armstrong, a boy, was running errands for the dives and honky-tonks of what was always presented to me as one of the most wicked of cities—to this day, whenever I think of New Orleans, I also helplessly think of Sodom and Gomorrah. My father never mentioned Louis Armstrong, except to forbid us to play his records; but there was a picture of him on our wall for a long time. One of my father's strong-willed female relatives had placed it there and forbade my father to take it down. He never did, but he eventually maneuvered her out of the house and when, some years later, she was in trouble and near death, he refused to do anything to help her.

He was, I think, very handsome. I gather this from pho-
tographs and from my own memories of him, dressed in his
Sunday best and on his way to preach a sermon somewhere,
when I was little. Handsome, proud, and ingrown, "like a toe-
nail," somebody said. But he looked to me, as I grew older,
like pictures I had seen of African tribal chieftains: he really
should have been naked, with war-paint on and barbaric me-
mentos, standing among spears. He could be chilling in the
pulpit and indescribably cruel in his personal life and he was
certainly the most bitter man I have ever met; yet it must be
said that there was something else in him, buried in him, which
lent him his tremendous power and, even, a rather crushing
charm. It had something to do with his blackness, I think—he
was very black—with his blackness and his beauty, and with
the fact that he knew that he was black but did not know that
he was beautiful. He claimed to be proud of his blackness but
it had also been the cause of much humiliation and it had fixed
bleak boundaries to his life. He was not a young man when
we were growing up and he had already suffered many kinds
of ruin; in his outrageously demanding and protective way he
loved his children, who were black like him and menaced, like
him; and all these things sometimes showed in his face when
he tried, never to my knowledge with any success, to establish
contact with any of us. When he took one of his children on
his knee to play, the child always became fretful and began
to cry; when he tried to help one of us with our homework
the absolutely unabating tension which emanated from him
caused our minds and our tongues to become paralyzed, so
that he, scarcely knowing why, flew into a rage and the child,
not knowing why, was punished. If it ever entered his head to

bring a surprise home for his children, it was, almost unfailingly, the wrong surprise and even the big watermelons he often brought home on his back in the summertime led to the most appalling scenes. I do not remember, in all those years, that one of his children was ever glad to see him come home. From what I was able to gather of his early life, it seemed that this inability to establish contact with other people had always marked him and had been one of the things which had driven him out of New Orleans. There was something in him, therefore, groping and tentative, which was never expressed and which was buried with him. One saw it most clearly when he was facing new people and hoping to impress them. But he never did, not for long. We went from church to smaller and more improbable church, he found himself in less and less demand as a minister, and by the time he died none of his friends had come to see him for a long time. He had lived and died in an intolerable bitterness of spirit and it frightened me, as we drove him to the graveyard through those unquiet, ruined streets, to see how powerful and overflowing this bitterness could be and to realize that this bitterness now was mine.

When he died I had been away from home for a little over a year. In that year I had had time to become aware of the meaning of all my father's bitter warnings, had discovered the secret of his proudly pursed lips and rigid carriage: I had discovered the weight of white people in the world. I saw that this had been for my ancestors and now would be for me an awful thing to live with and that the bitterness which had helped to kill my father could also kill me.

He had been ill a long time—in the mind, as we now realized, reliving instances of his fantastic intransigence in the new light of his affliction and endeavoring to feel a sorrow for him which never, quite, came true. We had not known that he was being eaten up by paranoia, and the discovery that his cruelty, to our bodies and our minds, had been one of the symptoms of his illness was not, then, enough to enable us to forgive him. The younger children felt, quite simply, relief that he would not be coming home anymore. My mother's observation that it was he, after all, who had kept them alive all these years meant nothing because the problems of keeping children alive are not real for children. The older children felt, with my father gone, that they could invite their friends to the house without fear that their friends would be insulted or, as had sometimes happened with me, being told that their friends were in league with the devil and intended to rob our family of everything we owned. (I didn't fail to wonder, and it made me hate him, what on earth we owned that anybody else would want.)

His illness was beyond all hope of healing before anyone realized that he was ill. He had always been so strange and had lived, like a prophet, in such unimaginably close communion with the Lord that his long silences which were punctuated by moans and hallelujahs and snatches of old songs while he sat at the living-room window never seemed odd to us. It was not until he refused to eat because, he said, his family was trying to poison him that my mother was forced to accept as a fact what had, until then, been only an unwilling suspicion. When he was committed, it was discovered that he had tuberculosis and, as it turned out, the disease of his mind allowed the disease of his body to destroy him. For the doctors could not force him to eat, either, and, though he was fed intravenously, it was clear from the beginning that there was no hope for him.

In my mind's eye I could see him, sitting at the window, locked up in his terrors; hating and fearing every living soul including his children who had betrayed him, too, by reaching towards the world which had despised him. There were nine of us. I began to wonder what it could have felt like for such a man to have had nine children whom he could barely feed. He used to make little jokes about our poverty, which never, of course, seemed very funny to us; they could not have seemed very funny to him, either, or else our all too feeble response to them would never have caused such rages. He spent great energy and achieved, to our chagrin, no small amount of success in keeping us away from the people who surrounded us, people who had all-night rent parties to which we listened when we should have been sleeping, people who cursed and drank and flashed razor blades on Lenox Avenue. He could not understand why, if they had so much energy to spare, they could not use it to make their lives better. He treated almost everybody on our block with a most uncharitable asperity and neither they, nor, of course, their children were slow to reciprocate.

The only white people who came to our house were welfare workers and bill collectors. It was almost always my mother who dealt with them, for my father's temper, which was at the mercy of his pride, was never to be trusted. It was clear that he felt their very presence in his home to be a violation: this was conveyed by his carriage, almost ludicrously stiff, and by his voice, harsh and vindictively polite. When I was around nine or ten I wrote a play which was directed by a young, white schoolteacher, a woman, who then took an interest in me, and gave me books to read and, in order to corroborate my theatrical bent, decided to take me to see what she somewhat tactlessly referred to as "real" plays. Theater-going was forbidden in our house, but, with the really cruel intuitiveness of a child, I suspected that the color of this woman's skin would carry the day for me. When, at school, she suggested taking me to the theater, I did not, as I might have done if she had been a Negro, find a way of discouraging her, but agreed that she should pick me up at my house one evening. I then, very cleverly, left all the rest to my mother, who suggested to my father, as I knew she would, that it would not be very nice to let such a kind woman make the trip for nothing. Also, since it was a schoolteacher, I imagine that my mother countered the idea of sin with the idea of "education," which word, even with my father, carried a kind of bitter weight.

Before the teacher came my father took me aside to ask *why* she was coming, what *interest* she could possibly have in our house, in a boy like me. I said I didn't know but I, too, suggested that it had something to do with education. And I understood that my father was waiting for me to say something—I didn't quite know what; perhaps that I wanted his protection against this teacher and her "education." I said none of these things and the teacher came and we went out. It was clear, during the brief interview in our living room, that my father was agreeing very much against his will and that he would have refused permission if he had dared. The fact that he did not dare caused me to despise him: I had no way of knowing that he was facing in that living room a wholly unprecedented and frightening situation.

Later, when my father had been laid off from his job, this woman became very important to us. She was really a very sweet and generous woman and went to a great deal of trouble to be of help to us, particularly during one awful winter. My mother called her by the highest name she knew: she said she was a "christian." My father could scarcely disagree but during the four or five years of our relatively close association he never trusted her and was always trying to surprise in her open, Midwestern face the genuine, cunningly hidden, and hideous motivation. In later years, particularly when it began to be clear that this "education" of mine was going to lead me to perdition, he became more explicit and warned me that my white friends in high school were not really my friends and that I would see, when I was older, how white people would do anything to keep a Negro down. Some of them could be nice, he admitted, but none of them were to be trusted and most of them were not even nice. The best thing was to have as little to do with them as possible. I did not feel this way and I was certain, in my innocence, that I never would.

But the year which preceded my father's death had made a great change in my life. I had been living in New Jersey, working in defense plants, working and living among southerners, white and black. I knew about the south, of course, and about how southerners treated Negroes and how they expected them to behave, but it had never entered my mind that anyone would look at me and expect *me* to behave that way. I learned in New Jersey that to be a Negro meant, precisely, that one was never looked at but was simply at the mercy of the reflexes the color of one's skin caused in other people. I acted in New Jersey as I had always acted, that is as though I thought a great deal of myself—I had to *act* that way—with results that were, simply, unbelievable. I had scarcely arrived

before I had earned the enmity, which was extraordinarily in-
genious, of all my superiors and nearly all my co-workers. In
the beginning, to make matters worse, I simply did not know
what was happening. I did not know what I had done, and I
shortly began to wonder what *anyone* could possibly do, to
bring about such unanimous, active, and unbearably vocal
hostility. I knew about jim-crow but I had never experienced
it. I went to the same self-service restaurant three times and
stood with all the Princeton boys before the counter, waiting
for a hamburger and coffee; it was always an extraordinarily
long time before anything was set before me; but it was not
until the fourth visit that I learned that, in fact, nothing had
ever been set before me: I had simply picked something up.
Negroes were not served there, I was told, and they had been
waiting for me to realize that I was always the only Negro
present. Once I was told this, I determined to go there all
the time. But now they were ready for me and, though some
dreadful scenes were subsequently enacted in that restaurant, I never ate there again.

It was the same story all over New Jersey, in bars, bowl-
ing alleys, diners, places to live. I was always being forced
to leave, silently, or with mutual imprecations. I very shortly
became notorious and children giggled behind me when I
passed and their elders whispered or shouted—they really
believed that I was mad. And it did begin to work on my
mind, of course; I began to be afraid to go anywhere and to
compensate for this I went places to which I really should not
have gone and where, God knows, I had no desire to be. My
reputation in town naturally enhanced my reputation at work
and my working day became one long series of acrobatics
designed to keep me out of trouble. I cannot say that these

acrobatics succeeded. It began to seem that the machinery of the organization I worked for was turning over, day and night, with but one aim: to eject me. I was fired once, and contrived, with the aid of a friend from New York, to get back on the payroll; was fired again, and bounced back again. It took a while to fire me for the third time, but the third time took. There were no loopholes anywhere. There was not even any way of getting back inside the gates.

That year in New Jersey lives in my mind as though it were the year during which, having an unsuspected predilection for it, I first contracted some dread, chronic disease, the unfailing symptom of which is a kind of blind fever, a pounding in the skull and fire in the bowels. Once this disease is contracted, one can never be really carefree again, for the fever, without an instant's warning, can recur at any moment. It can wreck more important things than race relations. There is not a Negro alive who does not have this rage in his blood— one has the choice, merely, of living with it consciously or surrendering to it. As for me, this fever has recurred in me, and does, and will until the day I die.

My last night in New Jersey, a white friend from New York took me to the nearest big town, Trenton, to go to the movies and have a few drinks. As it turned out, he also saved me from, at the very least, a violent whipping. Almost every detail of that night stands out very clearly in my memory. I even remember the name of the movie we saw because its title impressed me as being so patly ironical. It was a movie about the German occupation of France, starring Maureen O'Hara and Charles Laughton and called *This Land Is Mine*. I remember the name of the diner we walked into when the movie ended: it was the "American Diner." When we walked in the counterman asked what we wanted and I remember answering with the casual sharpness which had become my habit: "We want a hamburger and a cup of coffee, what do you think we want?" I do not know why, after a year of such rebuffs, I so completely failed to anticipate his answer, which was, of course, "We don't serve Negroes here." This reply failed to discompose me, at least for the moment. I made some sardonic comment about the name of the diner and we walked out into the streets.

This was the time of what was called the "brown-out," when the lights in all American cities were very dim. When we re-entered the streets something happened to me which had the force of an optical illusion, or a nightmare. The streets were very crowded and I was facing north. People were moving in every direction but it seemed to me, in that instant, that all of the people I could see, and many more than that, were moving toward me, against me, and that everyone was white. I remember how their faces gleamed. And I felt, like a physical sensation, a *click* at the nape of my neck as though some interior string connecting my head to my body had been cut. I began to walk. I heard my friend call after me, but I ignored him. Heaven only knows what was going on in his mind, but he had the good sense not to touch me—I don't know what would have happened if he had—and to keep me in sight. I don't know what was going on in my mind, either; I certainly had no conscious plan. I wanted to do something to crush these white faces, which were crushing me. I walked for perhaps a block or two until I came to an enormous, glittering, and fashionable restaurant in which I knew not even the intercession of the Virgin would cause me to be served. I pushed through the doors and took the first vacant seat I saw, at a table for two, and waited.

I do not know how long I waited and I rather wonder, until today, what I could possibly have looked like. Whatever I looked like, I frightened the waitress who shortly appeared, and the moment she appeared all of my fury flowed towards her. I hated her for her white face, and for her great, astounded, frightened eyes. I felt that if she found a black man so frightening I would make her fright worth-while.

She did not ask me what I wanted, but repeated, as though she had learned it somewhere, "We don't serve Negroes here." She did not say it with the blunt, derisive hostility to which I had grown so accustomed, but, rather, with a note of apology in her voice, and fear. This made me colder and more murderous than ever. I felt I had to do something with my hands. I wanted her to come close enough for me to get her neck between my hands.

So I pretended not to have understood her, hoping to draw her closer. And she did step a very short step closer, with her pencil poised incongruously over her pad, and repeated the formula: ". . . don't serve Negroes here."

Somehow, with the repetition of that phrase, which was already ringing in my head like a thousand bells of a nightmare, I realized that she would never come any closer and that I would have to strike from a distance. There was nothing on the table but an ordinary water-mug half full of water, and I picked this up and hurled it with all my strength at her. She ducked and it missed her and shattered against the mirror behind the bar. And, with that sound, my frozen blood abruptly thawed, I returned from wherever I had been, I *saw,* for the first time, the restaurant, the people with their mouths open, already, as it seemed to me, rising as one man, and I realized what I had done, and where I was, and I was frightened. I rose and began running for the door. A round, potbellied man grabbed me by the nape of the neck just as I reached the doors and began to beat me about the face. I kicked him and got loose and ran into the streets. My friend whispered, *"Run!"* and I ran.

My friend stayed outside the restaurant long enough to misdirect my pursuers and the police, who arrived, he told me, at once. I do not know what I said to him when he came to my room that night. I could not have said much. I felt, in the oddest, most awful way, that I had somehow betrayed him. I lived it over and over and over again, the way one relives an automobile accident after it has happened and one finds oneself alone and safe. I could not get over two facts, both equally difficult for the imagination to grasp, and one was that I could have been murdered. But the other was that I had been ready to commit murder. I saw nothing very clearly but I did see this: that my life, my *real* life, was in danger, and not from anything other people might do but from the hatred I carried in my own heart.

II

I had returned home around the second week in June—in great haste because it seemed that my father's death and my mother's confinement were both but a matter of hours. In the case of my mother, it soon became clear that she had simply made a miscalculation. This had always been her tendency and I don't believe that a single one of us arrived in the world, or has since arrived anywhere else, on time. But none of us dawdled so intolerably about the business of being born as did my baby sister. We sometimes amused ourselves, during those endless, stifling weeks, by picturing the baby sitting within in the safe, warm dark, bitterly regretting the necessity of becoming a part of our chaos and stubbornly putting it off as long as possible. I understood her perfectly and congratulated her on showing such good sense so soon. Death, however, sat as purposefully at my father's bedside as life stirred within my mother's womb and it was harder to understand why he so lingered in that long shadow. It seemed that he had bent, and for a long time, too, all of his energies towards dying. Now death was ready for him but my father held back.

All of Harlem, indeed, seemed to be infected by waiting. I had never before known it to be so violently still. Racial tensions throughout this country were exacerbated during the early years of the war, partly because the labor market brought together hundreds of thousands of ill-prepared people and partly because Negro soldiers, regardless of where they were born, received their military training in the south. What happened in defense plants and army camps had repercussions, naturally, in every Negro ghetto. The situation in Harlem had grown bad enough for clergymen, policemen, educators, politicians, and social workers to assert in one breath that there was no "crime wave" and to offer, in the very next breath, suggestions as to how to combat it. These suggestions always seemed to involve playgrounds, despite the fact that racial skirmishes were occurring in the playgrounds, too. Playground or not, crime wave or not, the Harlem police force had been augmented in March, and the unrest grew—

perhaps, in fact, partly as a result of the ghetto's instinctive hatred of policemen. Perhaps the most revealing news item, out of the steady parade of reports of muggings, stabbings, shootings, assaults, gang wars, and accusations of police brutality, is the item concerning six Negro girls who set upon a white girl in the subway because, as they all too accurately put it, she was stepping on their toes. Indeed she was, all over the nation.

I had never before been so aware of policemen, on foot, on horseback, on corners, everywhere, always two by two. Nor had I ever been so aware of small knots of people. They were on stoops and on corners and in doorways, and what was striking about them, I think, was that they did not seem to be talking. Never, when I passed these groups, did the usual sound of a curse or a laugh ring out and neither did there seem to be any hum of gossip. There was certainly, on the other hand, occurring between them communication extraordinarily intense. Another thing that was striking was the unexpected diversity of the people who made up these groups. Usually, for example, one would see a group of sharpies standing on the street corner, jiving the passing chicks; or a group of older men, usually, for some reason, in the vicinity of a barber shop, discussing baseball scores, or the numbers, or making rather chilling observations about women they had known. Women, in a general way, tended to be seen less often together—unless they were church women, or very young girls, or prostitutes met together for an unprofessional instant. But that summer I saw the strangest combinations: large, respectable, churchly matrons standing on the stoops or the corners with their hair tied up, together with a girl in sleazy satin whose face bore the marks of gin and the razor, or heavy-set, abrupt, no-nonsense older men, in company with the most disreputable and fanatical "race" men, or these same "race" men with the sharpies, or these sharpies with the churchly women. Seventh Day Adventists and Methodists and Spiritualists seemed to be hobnobbing with Holyrollers and they were all, alike, entangled with the most flagrant disbelievers; something heavy in their stance seemed to indicate that they had all, incredibly, seen a common vision, and on each face there seemed to be the same strange, bitter shadow.

The churchly women and the matter-of-fact, no-nonsense men had children in the Army. The sleazy girls they talked to had lovers there, the sharpies and the "race" men had friends and brothers there. It would have demanded an unquestioning patriotism, happily as uncommon in this country as it is undesirable, for these people not to have been disturbed by the bitter letters they received, by the newspaper stories they read, not to have been enraged by the posters, then to be found all over New York, which described the Japanese as "yellow-bellied Japs." It was only the "race" men, to be sure, who spoke ceaselessly of being revenged—how this vengeance was to be exacted was not clear—for the indignities and dangers suffered by Negro boys in uniform; but everybody felt a directionless, hopeless bitterness, as well as that panic which can scarcely be suppressed when one knows that a human being one loves is beyond one's reach, and in danger. This helplessness and this gnawing uneasiness does something, at length, to even the toughest mind. Perhaps the best way to sum all this up is to say that the people I knew felt, mainly, a peculiar kind of relief when they knew that their boys were being shipped out of the south, to do battle overseas. It was, perhaps, like feeling that the most dangerous part of a dangerous journey had been passed and that now, even if death should come, it would come with honor and without the complicity of their countrymen. Such a death would be, in short, a fact with which one could hope to live.

It was on the 28th of July, which I believe was a Wednesday, that I visited my father for the first time during his illness and for the last time in his life. The moment I saw him I knew why I had put off this visit so long. I had told my mother that I did not want to see him because I hated him. But this was not true. It was only that I *had* hated him and I wanted to hold on to this hatred. I did not want to look on him as a ruin: it was not a ruin I had hated. I imagine that one of the reasons people cling to their hates so stubbornly is because they sense, once hate is gone, that they will be forced to deal with pain.

We traveled out to him, his older sister and myself, to what seemed to be the very end of a very Long Island. It was hot and dusty and we wrangled, my aunt and I, all the way out, over the fact that I had recently begun to smoke and, as she said, to give myself airs. But I knew that she wrangled with me because she could not bear to face the fact of her brother's dying. Neither could I endure the reality of her despair, her unstated bafflement as to what had happened to her brother's life, and her own. So we wrangled and I smoked and from time to time she fell into a heavy reverie. Covertly, I watched her face, which was the face of an old woman; it had fallen in, the eyes were sunken and lightless; soon she would be dying, too.

In my childhood—it had not been so long ago—I had thought her beautiful. She had been quick-witted and quick-moving and very generous with all the children and each of

her visits had been an event. At one time one of my brothers and myself had thought of running away to live with her.
Now she could no longer produce out of her handbag some
unexpected and yet familiar delight. She made me feel pity
and revulsion and fear. It was awful to realize that she no
longer caused me to feel affection. The closer we came to
the hospital the more querulous she became and at the same
time, naturally, grew more dependent on me. Between pity
and guilt and fear I began to feel that there was another me
trapped in my skull like a jack-in-the-box who might escape
my control at any moment and fill the air with screaming.

She began to cry the moment we entered the room and
she saw him lying there, all shriveled and still, like a little
black monkey. The great, gleaming apparatus which fed him
and would have compelled him to be still even if he had been
able to move brought to mind, not beneficence, but torture;
the tubes entering his arm made me think of pictures I had
seen when a child, of Gulliver, tied down by the pygmies on
that island. My aunt wept and wept, there was a whistling
sound in my father's throat; nothing was said; he could not
speak. I wanted to take his hand, to say something. But I
do not know what I could have said, even if he could have
heard me. He was not really in that room with us, he had
at last really embarked on his journey; and though my aunt
told me that he said he was going to meet Jesus, I did not
hear anything except that whistling in his throat. The doctor
came back and we left, into that unbearable train again, and
home. In the morning came the telegram saying that he was
dead. Then the house was suddenly full of relatives, friends,
hysteria, and confusion and I quickly left my mother and
the children to the care of those impressive women, who, in

Negro communities at least, automatically appear at times of bereavement armed with lotions, proverbs, and patience, and an ability to cook. I went downtown. By the time I returned, later the same day, my mother had been carried to the hospital and the baby had been born.

III

For my father's funeral I had nothing black to wear and this posed a nagging problem all day long. It was one of those problems, simple, or impossible of solution, to which the mind insanely clings in order to avoid the mind's real trouble. I spent most of that day at the downtown apartment of a girl I knew, celebrating my birthday with whiskey and wondering what to wear that night. When planning a birthday celebration one naturally does not expect that it will be up against competition from a funeral and this girl had anticipated taking me out that night, for a big dinner and a night club afterwards. Sometime during the course of that long day we decided that we would go out anyway, when my father's funeral service was over. I imagine *I* decided it, since, as the funeral hour approached, it became clearer and clearer to me that I would not know what to do with myself when it was over. The girl, stifling her very lively concern as to the possible effects of the whiskey on one of my father's chief mourners, concentrated on being conciliatory and practically helpful. She found a black shirt for me somewhere and ironed it and, dressed in the darkest pants and jacket I owned, and slightly drunk, I made my way to my father's funeral.

The chapel was full, but not packed, and very quiet. There were, mainly, my father's relatives, and his children, and here and there I saw faces I had not seen since childhood, the faces of my father's one-time friends. They were very dark and solemn now, seeming somehow to suggest that they had known all along that something like this would happen. Chief among the mourners was my aunt, who had quarreled with my father all his life; by which I do not mean to suggest that her mourning was insincere or that she had not loved him. I suppose that she was one of the few people in the world who had, and their incessant quarreling proved precisely the strength of the tie that bound them. The only other person in the world, as far as I knew, whose relationship to my father rivaled my aunt's in depth was my mother, who was not there.

It seemed to me, of course, that it was a very long funeral. But it was, if anything, a rather shorter funeral than most, nor, since there were no overwhelming, uncontrollable expressions of grief, could it be called—if I dare to use the word— successful. The minister who preached my father's funeral sermon was one of the few my father had still been seeing as he neared his end. He presented to us in his sermon a man whom none of us had ever seen—a man thoughtful, patient, and forbearing, a Christian inspiration to all who knew him, and a model for his children. And no doubt the children, in their disturbed and guilty state, were almost ready to believe this; he had been remote enough to be anything and, anyway, the shock of the incontrovertible, that it was really our father lying up there in that casket, prepared the mind for anything. His sister moaned and this grief-stricken moaning was taken as corroboration. The other faces held a dark, non-committal thoughtfulness. This was not the man they had known, but they had scarcely expected to be confronted with *him;* this was, in a sense deeper than questions of fact, the man they

had not known, and the man they had not known may have
been the real one. The real man, whoever he had been, had
suffered and now he was dead: this was all that was sure and
all that mattered now. Every man in the chapel hoped that
when his hour came he, too, would be eulogized, which is
to say forgiven, and that all of his lapses, greeds, errors, and
strayings from the truth would be invested with coherence
and looked upon with charity. This was perhaps the last thing
human beings could give each other and it was what they
demanded, after all, of the Lord. Only the Lord saw the midnight tears, only He was present when one of His children,
moaning and wringing hands, paced up and down the room.
When one slapped one's child in anger the recoil in the heart
reverberated through heaven and became part of the pain of
the universe. And when the children were hungry and sullen
and distrustful and one watched them, daily, growing wilder,
and further away, and running headlong into danger, it was
the Lord who knew what the charged heart endured as the
strap was laid to the backside; the Lord alone who knew what
one *would* have said if one had had, like the Lord, the gift
of the living word. It was the Lord who knew of the impossibility every parent in that room faced: how to prepare the
child for the day when the child would be despised and how
to *create* in the child—by what means?—a stronger antidote
to this poison than one had found for oneself. The avenues,
side streets, bars, billiard halls, hospitals, police stations,
and even the playgrounds of Harlem—not to mention the
houses of correction, the jails, and the morgue—testified to
the potency of the poison while remaining silent as to the ef-
ficacy of whatever antidote, irresistibly raising the question
of whether or not such an antidote existed; raising, which

was worse, the question of whether or not an antidote was desirable; perhaps poison should be fought with poison. With these several schisms in the mind and with more terrors in the heart than could be named, it was better not to judge the man who had gone down under an impossible burden. It was better to remember: *Thou knowest this man's fall; but thou knowest not his wrassling.*

While the preacher talked and I watched the children— years of changing their diapers, scrubbing them, slapping them, taking them to school, and scolding them had had the perhaps inevitable result of making me love them, though I am not sure I knew this then—my mind was busily breaking out with a rash of disconnected impressions. Snatches of popular songs, indecent jokes, bits of books I had read, movie sequences, faces, voices, political issues—I thought I was going mad; all these impressions suspended, as it were, in the solution of the faint nausea produced in me by the heat and liquor. For a moment I had the impression that my alcoholic breath, inefficiently disguised with chewing gum, filled the entire chapel. Then someone began singing one of my father's favorite songs and, abruptly, I was with him, sitting on his knee, in the hot, enormous, crowded church which was the first church we attended. It was the Abyssinia Baptist Church on 138th Street. We had not gone there long. With this image, a host of others came. I had forgotten, in the rage of my growing up, how proud my father had been of me when I was little. Apparently, I had had a voice and my father had liked to show me off before the members of the church. I had forgotten what he had looked like when he was pleased but now I remembered that he had always been grinning with pleasure when my solos ended. I even remembered certain expressions on his face when he teased my mother—had he loved her? I would never know. And when had it all begun to change? For now it seemed that he had not always been cruel. I remembered being taken for a haircut and scraping my knee on the footrest of the barber's chair and I remembered my father's face as he soothed my crying and applied the stinging iodine. Then I remembered our fights, fights which had been of the worst possible kind because my technique had been silence.

I remembered the one time in all our life together when we had really spoken to each other.

It was on a Sunday and it must have been shortly before I left home. We were walking, just the two of us, in our usual silence, to or from church. I was in high school and had been doing a lot of writing and I was, at about this time, the editor of the high school magazine. But I had also been a Young Minister and had been preaching from the pulpit. Lately, I had been taking fewer engagements and preached as rarely as possible. It was said in the church, quite truthfully, that I was "cooling off."

My father asked me abruptly, "You'd rather write than preach, wouldn't you?"

I was astonished at his question—because it was a real question. I answered, "Yes."

That was all we said. It was awful to remember that that was all we had *ever* said.

The casket now was opened and the mourners were being led up the aisle to look for the last time on the deceased. The assumption was that the family was too overcome with grief to be allowed to make this journey alone and I watched while my aunt was led to the casket and, muffled in black,

and shaking, led back to her seat. I disapproved of forcing
the children to look on their dead father, considering that the
shock of his death, or, more truthfully, the shock of death as
a reality, was already a little more than a child could bear, but
my judgment in this matter had been overruled and there
they were, bewildered and frightened and very small, being
led, one by one, to the casket. But there is also something
very gallant about children at such moments. It has something to do with their silence and gravity and with the fact
that one cannot help them. Their legs, somehow, seem *ex-
posed,* so that it is at once incredible and terribly clear that
their legs are all they have to hold them up.

I had not wanted to go to the casket myself and I certainly had not wished to be led there, but there was no way
of avoiding either of these forms. One of the deacons led
me up and I looked on my father's face. I cannot say that it
looked like him at all. His blackness had been equivocated
by powder and there was no suggestion in that casket of what
his power had or could have been. He was simply an old man
dead, and it was hard to believe that he had ever given anyone either joy or pain. Yet, his life filled that room. Further
up the avenue his wife was holding his newborn child. Life
and death so close together, and love and hatred, and right
and wrong, said something to me which I did not want to
hear concerning man, concerning the life of man.

After the funeral, while I was downtown desperately celebrating my birthday, a Negro soldier, in the lobby of the
Hotel Braddock, got into a fight with a white policeman over
a Negro girl. Negro girls, white policemen, in or out of uniform, and Negro males—in or out of uniform—were part of
the furniture of the lobby of the Hotel Braddock and this was

certainly not the first time such an incident had occurred. It was destined, however, to receive an unprecedented publicity, for the fight between the policeman and the soldier ended with the shooting of the soldier. Rumor, flowing immediately to the streets outside, stated that the soldier had been shot in the back, an instantaneous and revealing invention, and that the soldier had died protecting a Negro woman. The facts were somewhat different—for example, the soldier had not been shot in the back, and was not dead, and the girl seems to have been as dubious a symbol of womanhood as her white counterpart in Georgia usually is, but no one was interested in the facts. They preferred the invention because this invention expressed and corroborated their hates and fears so perfectly. It is just as well to remember that people are always doing this. Perhaps many of those legends, including Christianity, to which the world clings began their conquest of the world with just some such concerted surrender to distortion. The effect, in Harlem, of this particular legend was like the effect of a lit match in a tin of gasoline. The mob gathered before the doors of the Hotel Braddock simply began to swell and to spread in every direction, and Harlem exploded.

The mob did not cross the ghetto lines. It would have been easy, for example, to have gone over Morningside Park on the west side or to have crossed the Grand Central railroad tracks at 125th Street on the east side, to wreak havoc in white neighborhoods. The mob seems to have been mainly interested in something more potent and real than the white face, that is, in white power, and the principal damage done during the riot of the summer of 1943 was to white business establishments in Harlem. It might have been a far bloodier story, of course, if, at the hour the riot began, these

establishments had still been open. From the Hotel Braddock the mob fanned out, east and west along 125th Street,
and for the entire length of Lenox, Seventh, and Eighth avenues. Along each of these avenues, and along each major
side street—116th, 125th, 135th, and so on—bars, stores,
pawnshops, restaurants, even little luncheonettes had been
smashed open and entered and looted—looted, it might be
added, with more haste than efficiency. The shelves really
looked as though a bomb had struck them. Cans of beans
and soup and dog food, along with toilet paper, corn flakes,
sardines and milk tumbled every which way, and abandoned
cash registers and cases of beer leaned crazily out of the
splintered windows and were strewn along the avenues.
Sheets, blankets, and clothing of every description formed
a kind of path, as though people had dropped them while
running. I truly had not realized that Harlem *had* so many
stores until I saw them all smashed open; the first time the
word *wealth* ever entered my mind in relation to Harlem was
when I saw it scattered in the streets. But one's first, incon-
gruous impression of plenty was countered immediately by
an impression of waste. None of this was doing anybody any
good. It would have been better to have left the plate glass as
it had been and the goods lying in the stores.

It would have been better, but it would also have been
intolerable, for Harlem had needed something to smash. To
smash something is the ghetto's chronic need. Most of the
time it is the members of the ghetto who smash each other,
and themselves. But as long as the ghetto walls are standing there will always come a moment when these outlets do
not work. That summer, for example, it was not enough to
get into a fight on Lenox Avenue, or curse out one's cronies

in the barber shops. If ever, indeed, the violence which fills Harlem's churches, pool halls, and bars erupts outward in a more direct fashion, Harlem and its citizens are likely to vanish in an apocalyptic flood. That this is not likely to happen is due to a great many reasons, most hidden and powerful among them the Negro's real relation to the white American. This relation prohibits, simply, anything as uncomplicated and satisfactory as pure hatred. In order really to hate white people, one has to blot so much out of the mind—and the heart—that this hatred itself becomes an exhausting and self-destructive pose. But this does not mean, on the other hand, that love comes easily: the white world is too powerful, too complacent, too ready with gratuitous humiliation, and, above all, too ignorant and too innocent for that. One is absolutely forced to make perpetual qualifications and one's own reactions are always canceling each other out. It is this, really, which has driven so many people mad, both white and black. One is always in the position of having to decide between amputation and gangrene. Amputation is swift but time may prove that the amputation was not necessary—or one may delay the amputation too long. Gangrene is slow, but it is impossible to be sure that one is reading one's symptoms right. The idea of going through life as a cripple is more than one can bear, and equally unbearable is the risk of swelling up slowly, in agony, with poison. And the trouble, finally, is that the risks are real even if the choices do not exist.

"But as for me and my house," my father had said, "we will serve the Lord." I wondered, as we drove him to his resting place, what this line had meant for him. I had heard him preach it many times. I had preached it once myself, proudly giving it an interpretation different from my father's. Now the whole thing came back to me, as though my father and I were on our way to Sunday school and I were memorizing the golden text: *And if it seem evil unto you to serve the Lord, choose you this day whom you will serve; whether the gods which your fathers served that were on the other side of the flood, or the gods of the Amorites, in whose land ye dwell: but as for me and my house, we will serve the Lord.* I suspected in these familiar lines a meaning which had never been there for me before. All of my father's texts and songs, which I had decided were meaningless, were arranged before me at his death like empty bottles, waiting to hold the meaning which life would give them for me. This was his legacy: nothing is ever escaped. That bleakly memorable morning I hated the unbelievable streets and the Negroes and whites who had, equally, made them that way. But I knew that it was folly, as my father would have said, this bitterness was folly. It was necessary to hold on to the things that mattered. The dead man mattered, the new life mattered; blackness and whiteness did not matter; to believe that they did was to acquiesce in one's own destruction. Hatred, which could destroy so much, never failed to destroy the man who hated and this was an immutable law.

It began to seem that one would have to hold in the mind forever two ideas which seemed to be in opposition. The first idea was acceptance, the acceptance, totally without rancor, of life as it is, and men as they are: in the light of this idea, it goes without saying that injustices is a commonplace. But this did not mean that one could be complacent, for the second idea was of equal power: that one must never, in one's own life, accept these injustices as commonplace but must fight them with all one's strength. This fight begins, however, in the heart and it now had been laid to my charge to keep my own heart free of hatred and despair. This intimation made my heart heavy and, now that my father was irrecoverable, I wished that he had been beside me so that I could have searched his face for the answers which only the future would give me now.

PART THREE

Encounter on the Seine: Black Meets Brown

In Paris nowadays it is rather more difficult for an American Negro to become a really successful entertainer than it is rumored to have been some thirty years ago. For one thing, champagne has ceased to be drunk out of slippers, and the frivolously colored thousand-franc note is neither as elastic nor as freely spent as it was in the 1920's. The musicians and singers who are here now must work very hard indeed to acquire the polish and style which will land them in the big time. Bearing witness to this eternally tantalizing possibility, performers whose eminence is unchallenged, like Duke Ellington or Louis Armstrong, occasionally pass through. Some of their ambitious followers are in or near the big time already; others are gaining reputations which have yet to be tested in the States. Gordon Heath, who will be remembered for his performances as the embattled soldier in Broadway's *Deep Are the Roots* some seasons back, sings ballads nightly in his own night club on the Rue L'Abbaye; and everyone who comes to Paris these days sooner or later discovers Chez Inez, a night club in the Latin Quarter run by a singer named Inez Cavanaugh, which specializes in fried chicken and jazz. It is at Chez Inez that many an unknown first performs in public, going on thereafter, if not always to greater triumphs, at least to other night clubs, and possibly landing a contract to tour the Riviera during the spring and summer.

In general, only the Negro entertainers are able to maintain a useful and unquestioning comradeship with other Negroes. Their nonperforming, colored countrymen are, nearly to a man, incomparably more isolated, and it must be conceded that this isolation is deliberate. It is estimated that there are five hundred American Negroes living in this city, the vast majority of them veterans studying on the G.I. Bill. They are studying everything from the Sorbonne's standard *Cours de Civilisation Française* to abnormal psychology, brain surgery, music, fine arts, and literature. Their isolation from each other is not difficult to understand if one bears in mind the axiom, unquestioned by American landlords, that Negroes are happy only when they are kept together. Those driven to break this pattern by leaving the U.S. ghettos not merely have effected a social and physical leave-taking but also have been precipitated into cruel psychological warfare. It is altogether inevitable that past humiliations should become associated not only with one's traditional oppressors but also with one's traditional kinfolk.

Thus the sight of a face from home is not invariably a source of joy, but can also quite easily become a source of embarrassment or rage. The American Negro in Paris is forced at last to exercise an undemocratic discrimination rarely practiced by Americans, that of judging his people, duck by duck, and distinguishing them one from another. Through this deliberate isolation, through lack of numbers, and above all through his own overwhelming need to be, as it were, forgotten, the American Negro in Paris is very nearly the invisible man.

The wariness with which he regards his colored kin is a natural extension of the wariness with which he regards all of his countrymen. At the beginning, certainly, he cherishes rather exaggerated hopes of the French. His white countrymen, by and large, fail to justify his fears, partly because the social climate does not encourage an outward display of racial bigotry, partly out of their awareness of being ambassadors, and finally, I should think, because they are themselves relieved at being no longer forced to think in terms of color. There remains, nevertheless, in the encounter of white Americans and Negro Americans the high potential of an awkward or an ugly situation.

The white American regards his darker brother through the distorting screen created by a lifetime of conditioning. He is accustomed to regard him either as a needy and deserving martyr or as the soul of rhythm, but he is more than a little intimidated to find this stranger so many miles from home. At first he tends instinctively, whatever his intelligence may belatedly clamor, to take it as a reflection on his personal honor and good-will; and at the same time, with that winning generosity, at once good-natured and uneasy, which characterizes Americans, he would like to establish communication, and sympathy, with his compatriot. "And how do *you* feel about it?" he would like to ask, "it" being anything—the Russians, Betty Grable, the Place de la Concorde. The trouble here is that any "it," so tentatively offered, may suddenly become loaded and vibrant with tension, creating in the air between the two thus met an intolerable atmosphere of danger.

The Negro, on the other hand, via the same conditioning which constricts the outward gesture of the whites, has
learned to anticipate: as the mouth opens he divines what
the tongue will utter. He has had time, too, long before he
came to Paris, to reflect on the absolute and personally expensive futility of taking any one of his countrymen to task
for his status in America, or of hoping to convey to them any
of his experience. The American Negro and white do not,
therefore, discuss the past, except in considerately guarded
snatches. Both are quite willing, and indeed quite wise, to
remark instead the considerably overrated impressiveness of
the Eiffel Tower.

The Eiffel Tower has naturally long since ceased to divert
the French, who consider that all Negroes arrive from America, trumpet-laden and twinkle-toed, bearing scars so unutterably painful that all of the glories of the French Republic
may not suffice to heal them. This indignant generosity poses
problems of its own, which, language and custom being what
they are, are not so easily averted.

The European tends to avoid the really monumental confusion which might result from an attempt to apprehend the
relationship of the forty-eight states to one another, clinging
instead to such information as is afforded by radio, press, and
film, to anecdotes considered to be illustrative of American
life, and to the myth that we have ourselves perpetuated. The
result, in conversation, is rather like seeing one's back yard
reproduced with extreme fidelity, but in such a perspective
that it becomes a place which one has never seen or visited,
which never has existed, and which never can exist. The Negro is forced to say "Yes" to many a difficult question, and yet
to deny the conclusion to which his answers seem to point.

His past, he now realizes, has not been simply a series of ropes and bonfires and humiliations, but something vastly more complex, which, as he thinks painfully, "It was much worse than that," was also, he irrationally feels, something much better. As it is useless to excoriate his countrymen, it is galling now to be pitied as a victim, to accept this ready sympathy which is limited only by its failure to accept him as an American. He finds himself involved, in another language, in the same old battle: the battle for his own identity. To accept the reality of his being an American becomes a matter involving his integrity and his greatest hopes, for only by accepting this reality can be hope to make articulate to himself or to others the uniqueness of his experience, and to set free the spirit so long anonymous and caged.

The ambivalence of his status is thrown into relief by his encounters with the Negro students from France's colonies who live in Paris. The French African comes from a region and a way of life which—at least from the American point of view—is exceedingly primitive, and where exploitation takes more naked forms. In Paris, the African Negro's status, conspicuous and subtly inconvenient, is that of a colonial; and he leads here the intangibly precarious life of someone abruptly and recently uprooted. His bitterness is unlike that of his American kinsman in that it is not so treacherously likely to be turned against himself. He has, not so very many miles away, a homeland to which his relationship, no less than his responsibility, is overwhelmingly clear: His country must be given—or it must seize—its freedom. This bitter ambition is shared by his fellow colonials, with whom he has a common language, and whom he has no wish whatever to avoid; without whose sustenance, indeed, he would be almost altogether lost in Paris. They live in groups together, in the same neighborhoods, in student hotels and under conditions which cannot fail to impress the American as almost unendurable.

Yet what the American is seeing is not simply the poverty of the student but the enormous gap between the European and American standards of living. *All* of the students in the Latin Quarter live in ageless, sinister-looking hotels; they are all forced continually to choose between cigarettes and cheese at lunch.

It is true that the poverty and anger which the American Negro sees must be related to Europe and not to America. Yet, as he wishes for a moment that he were home again, where at least the terrain is familiar, there begins to race within him, like the despised beat of the tom-tom, echoes of a past which he has not yet been able to utilize, intimations of a responsibility which he has not yet been able to face. He begins to conjecture how much he has gained and lost during his long sojourn in the American republic. The African before him has endured privation, injustice, medieval cruelty; but the African has not yet endured the utter alienation of himself from his people and his past. His mother did not sing "Sometimes I Feel Like a Motherless Child," and he has not, all his life long, ached for acceptance in a culture which pronounced straight hair and white skin the only acceptable beauty.

They face each other, the Negro and the African, over a gulf of three hundred years—an alienation too vast to be conquered in an evening's good-will, too heavy and too double-edged ever to be trapped in speech. This alienation causes the Negro to recognize that he is a hybrid. Not a physical hybrid merely: in every aspect of his living he betrays the memory of the auction block and the impact of the happy ending. In white Americans he finds reflected—repeated, as it were, in a higher key—his tensions, his terrors, his tenderness. Dimly and for the first time, there begins to fall into perspective the nature of the roles they have played in the lives and history of each other. Now he is bone of their bone, flesh of their flesh; they have loved and hated and obsessed and feared each other and his blood is in their soil. Therefore he cannot deny them, nor can they ever be divorced.

The American Negro cannot explain to the African what surely seems in himself to be a want of manliness, of racial pride, a maudlin ability to forgive. It is difficult to make clear that he is not seeking to forfeit his birthright as a black man, but that, on the contrary, it is precisely this birthright which he is struggling to recognize and make articulate. Perhaps it now occurs to him that in this need to establish himself in relation to his past he is most American, that this depthless alienation from oneself and one's people is, in sum, the American experience.

Yet one day he will face his home again; nor can he realistically expect to find overwhelming changes. In America, it is true, the appearance is perpetually changing, each generation greeting with short-lived exultation yet more dazzling additions to our renowned façade. But the ghetto, anxiety, bitterness, and guilt continue to breed their indescribable complex of tensions. What time will bring Americans is at last their own identity. It is on this dangerous voyage and in the same boat that the American Negro will make peace with himself and with the voiceless many thousands gone before him.

A Question of Identity

The American student colony in Paris is a social phenomenon so amorphous as to at once demand and defy the generality. One is far from being in the position of finding not enough to say—one finds far too much, and everything one finds is contradictory. What one wants to know at bottom, is what *they* came to find: to which question there are—at least—as many answers as there are faces at the café tables.

The assumed common denominator, which is their military experience, does not shed on this question as much light as one might hope. For one thing, it becomes impossible, the moment one thinks about it, to predicate the existence of a *common* experience. The moment one thinks about it, it becomes apparent that there is no such thing. That experience is a private, and a very largely speechless affair is the principal truth, perhaps, to which the colony under discussion bears witness—though the aggressively unreadable face which they, collectively, present also suggests the more disturbing possibility that experience may perfectly well be meaningless. This loaded speculation aside, it is certainly true that whatever this experience has done to them, or for them, whatever the effect has been, is, or will be, is a question to which no one has yet given any strikingly coherent answer. Military experience does not, furthermore, necessarily mean experience of battle, so that the student colony's common denominator reduces itself to nothing more than the fact that all of its members have spent some time in uniform. This is the common denominator of their entire generation, of which the majority is not to be found in Paris, or, for that matter, in Europe. One is at the outset, therefore, forbidden to assume that the fact of having surrendered to the necessary anonymity of uniform, or of having undergone the shock of battle, was enough to occasion this flight from home. The best that one can do by way of uniting these so disparate identities is simply to accept, without comment, the fact of their military experience, without questioning its extent; and, further, to suggest that they form, by virtue of their presence here, a somewhat unexpected minority. Unlike the majority of their fellows, who were simply glad to get back home, these have elected to tarry in the Old World, among scenes and people unimaginably removed from anything they have known. They are willing, apparently, at least for a season, to endure the wretched Parisian plumbing, the public baths, the Paris age, and dirt—to pursue some end, mysterious and largely inarticulate, arbitrarily summed up in the verb *to study*.

Arbitrarily, because, however hard the ex-GI is studying, it is very difficult to believe that it was only for this reason that he traveled so far. He is not, usually, studying anything which he couldn't study at home, in far greater comfort. (We are limiting ourselves, for the moment, to those people who are—more or less seriously—studying, as opposed to those, to be considered later, who are merely gold-bricking.) The people, for example, who are studying painting, which seems,

until one looks around, the best possible subject to be studying here, are not studying, after all, with Picasso, or Matisse—
they are studying with teachers of the same caliber as those
they would have found in the States. They are treated by
these teachers with the same highhandedness, and they accept their dicta with the very same measure of American salt.
Nor can it be said that they produce canvases of any greater
interest than those to be found along Washington Square, or
in the cold-water flats of New York's lower east side. There is,
au contraire, more than a little truth to the contention that
the east side has a certain edge over Montparnasse, and this
in spite of the justly renowned Paris light. If we tentatively
use—purely by virtue of his numbers—the student painter as
the nearest possible approach to a "typical" student, we find
that his motives for coming to Paris are anything but clear.
One is forced to suppose that it was nothing more than the
legend of Paris, not infrequently at its most vulgar and superficial level. It was certainly no love for French tradition, whatever, indeed, in his mind, that tradition may be; and, in any
case, since he is himself without a tradition, he is ill equipped
to deal with the traditions of any other people. It was no love
for their language, which he doesn't, beyond the most inescapable necessities, speak; nor was it any love for their history,
his grasp of French history being yet more feeble than his
understanding of his own. It was no love for the monuments,
cathedrals, palaces, shrines, for which, again, nothing in his
experience prepares him, and to which, when he is not totally
indifferent, he brings only the hurried bewilderment of the
tourist. It was not even any particular admiration, or sympathy for the French, or, at least, none strong enough to bear the
strain of actual contact. He may, at home, have admired their

movies, in which case, confronting the reality, he tends to feel a little taken in. Those images created by Marcel Carné, for example, prove themselves treacherous precisely because they are so exact. The sordid French hotel room, so admirably detailed by the camera, speaking, in its quaintness, and distance, so beautifully of romance, undergoes a sea-change, becomes a room positively hostile to romance, once it is oneself, and not Jean Gabin, who lives there. This is the difference, simply, between what one desires and what the reality insists on—which difference we will not pursue except to observe that, since the reasons which brought the student here are so romantic, and incoherent, he has come, in effect, to a city which exists only in his mind. He cushions himself, so it would seem, against the shock of reality, by refusing for a very long time to recognize Paris at all, but clinging instead to its image. This is the reason, perhaps, that Paris for so long fails to make any mark on him; and may also be why, when the tension between the real and the imagined can no longer be supported, so many people undergo a species of breakdown, or take the first boat home.

For Paris is, according to its legend, the city where everyone loses his head, and his morals, lives through at least one *histoire d'amour*, ceases, quite, to arrive anywhere on time, and thumbs his nose at the Puritans—the city, in brief, where all become drunken on the fine old air of freedom. This legend, in the fashion of legends, has this much to support it, that it is not at all difficult to see how it got started. It is limited, as legends are limited, by being—literally—unlivable, and by referring to the past. It is perhaps not amazing, therefore, that this legend appears to have virtually nothing to do with the life of Paris itself, with the lives, that is, of the natives, to whom the city, no less than the legend, belong. The charm of this legend proves itself capable of withstanding the most improbable excesses of the French bureaucracy, the weirdest vagaries of the *concierge*, the fantastic rents paid for uncomfortable apartments, the discomfort itself, and, even, the great confusion and despair which is reflected in French politics—and in French faces. More, the legend operates to place all of the inconveniences endured by the foreigner, to say nothing of the downright misery which is the lot of many of the natives, in the gentle glow of the picturesque, and the absurd; so that, finally, it is perfectly possible to be enamored of Paris while remaining totally indifferent, or even hostile to the French. And this is made possible by the one person in Paris whom the legend seems least to affect, who is not living it at all, that is, the Parisian himself. He, with his impenetrable *politesse*, and with techniques unspeakably more direct, keeps the traveler at an unmistakable arm's length. Unlucky indeed, as well as rare, the traveler who thirsts to know the lives of the people—the people don't want him in their lives. Neither does the Parisian exhibit the faintest personal interest, or curiosity, concerning the life, or habits, of any stranger. So long as he keeps within the law, which, after all, most people have sufficient ingenuity to do, he may stand on his head, for all the Parisian cares. It is this arrogant indifference on the part of the Parisian, with its unpredictable effects on the traveler, which makes so splendid the Paris air, to say nothing whatever of the exhilarating effect it has on the Paris scene.

The American student lives here, then, in a kind of social limbo. He is allowed, and he gratefully embraces irresponsibility; and, at the same time, since he is an American, he is invested with power, whether or not he likes it, however he may choose to confirm or deny it. Though the students of any nation, in Paris, are allowed irresponsibility, few seem to need it as desperately as Americans seem to need it; and none, naturally, move in the same aura of power, which sets up in the general breast a perceptible anxiety, and wonder, and a perceptible resentment. This is the "catch," for the American, in the Paris freedom: that he becomes here a kind of revenant to Europe, the future of which continent, it may be, is in his hands. The problems proceeding from the distinction he thus finds thrust upon him might not, for a sensibility less definitively lonely, frame so painful a dilemma: but the American wishes to be liked *as a person*, an implied distinction which makes perfect sense to him, and none whatever to the European. What the American means is that he does not want to be confused with the Marshall Plan, Hollywood, the Yankee dollar, television, or Senator McCarthy. What the European, in a thoroughly exasperating innocence, assumes is that the American cannot, of course, be divorced from the so diverse phenomena which make up his country, and that he is willing, and able, to clarify the American conundrum. If the American cannot do this, his despairing aspect seems to say, who, under heaven, can? This moment, which instinctive ingenuity delays as long as possible, nevertheless arrives, and punctuates the Paris honeymoon. It is the moment, so to speak, when one leaves the Paris of legend and finds oneself in the real and difficult Paris of the present. At this moment Paris ceases to be a city dedicated to *la vie bohème*, and becomes one of the cities of Europe. At this point, too, it may be suggested, the legend of Paris has done its deadly work, which is, perhaps, so to stun the traveler with freedom that

he begins to long for the prison of home—home then becoming the place where questions are not asked.

It is at this point, precisely, that many and many a student
packs his bags for home. The transformation which can be
effected, in less than a year, in the attitude and aspirations
of the youth who has divorced himself from the crudities of
main street in order to be married with European finesse is,
to say the very least, astounding. His brief period of enchant-
ment having ended, he cannot wait, it seems, to look again
on his native land—the virtues of which, if not less crude,
have also become, abruptly, *simple*, and *vital*. With the air of
a man who has but barely escaped tumbling headlong into
the bottomless pit, he tells you that he can scarcely wait to
leave this city, which has been revealed to the eye of his
maturity as old, dirty, crumbling, and dead. The people who
were, when he arrived at Le Havre, the heirs of the world's
richest culture, the possessors of the world's largest *esprit*,
are really decadent, penurious, self-seeking, and false, with
no trace of American spontaneity, and lacking in the least
gratitude for American favors. Only America is alive, only
Americans are doing anything worth mentioning in the arts,
or in any other field of human activity: to America, only, the
future belongs. Whereas, but only yesterday, to confess a
fondness for anything American was to be suspected of the
most indefensible jingoism, to suggest today that Europe is
not all black is to place oneself under the suspicion of harboring treasonable longings. The violence of his embrace
of things American is embarrassing, not only because one
is not quite prepared to follow his admirable example, but
also because it is impossible not to suspect that his present
acceptance of his country is no less romantic, and unreal,

than his earlier rejection. It is as easy, after all, and as meaningless, to embrace uncritically the cultural sterility of main
street as it is to decry it. Both extremes avoid the question of
whether or not main street is really sterile, avoid, in fact—
which is the principal convenience of extremes—any questions about main street at all. What one vainly listens for in
this cacophony of affirmation is any echo, however faint of
individual maturity. It is really quite impossible to be affirmative about anything which one refuses to question; one
is doomed to remain inarticulate about anything which one
hasn't, by an act of the imagination, made one's own. This so
suddenly affirmative student is but changing the fashion of
his innocence, nothing being more improbable than that he
is now prepared, as he insists, to embrace his Responsibilities—the very word, in the face of his monumental aversion
to experience, seems to shrink to the dimensions of a new,
and rather sinister, frivolity.

The student, homeward bound, has only chosen, however,
to flee down the widest road. Of those who remain here, the
majority have taken roads more devious, and incomparably
better hidden—so well hidden that they themselves are lost.
    One very often finds in this category that student whose
adaptation to French life seems to have been most perfect,
and whose studies—of French art, or the drama, the language, or the history—give him the greatest right to be here.
This student has put aside chewing gum forever, he eschews
the T-shirt, and the crew cut, he can only with difficulty be
prevailed upon to see an American movie, and it is so patent
that he is *actually* studying that his appearance at the café

tables is never taken as evidence of frivolity, but only as proof
of his admirable passion to study the customs of the country.
One assumes that he is living as the French live—which assumption, however, is immediately challenged by the suspicion that no American can live as the French live, even if one
could find an American who wanted to. This student lives,
nevertheless, with a French family, with whom he speaks
French, and takes his meals; and he knows, as some students
do not, that the Place de la Bastille no longer holds the prison.
He has read, or is reading, all of Racine, Proust, Gide, Sar-
tre, and authors more obscure—in the original, naturally. He
regularly visits the museums, and he considers Arletty to be
the most beautiful woman and the finest actress in the world.
But the world, it seems, has become the French world: he is
unwilling to recognize any other. This so severely cramps the
American conversational style, that one looks on this student
with awe, and some shame—he is so spectacularly getting out
of his European experience everything it has to give. He has
certainly made contact with the French, and isn't wasting his
time in Paris talking to people he might perfectly well have
met in America. His friends are French, in the classroom, in
the bistro, on the boulevard, and, of course, at home—it is
only that one is sometimes driven to wonder what on earth
they find to talk about. This wonder is considerably increased
when, in the rare conversations he condescends to have in
English, one discovers that, certain picturesque details aside,
he seems to know no more about life in Paris than everybody
knew at home. His friends have, it appears, leaped unscathed
from the nineteenth into the twentieth century, entirely un-
dismayed by any of the reverses suffered by their country.
This makes them a remarkable band indeed, but it is in vain

that one attempts to discover anything more about them—
their conversation being limited, one gathers, to remarks
about French wine, witticisms concerning l'amour, French
history, and the glories of Paris. The remarkably limited range
of their minds is matched only by their perplexing definition
of friendship, a definition which does not seem to include
any suggestion of communication, still less of intimacy. Since,
in short, the relationship of this perfectly adapted student to
the people he now so strenuously adores is based simply on
his unwillingness to allow them any of the human attributes
with which his countrymen so confounded him at home, and
since his vaunted grasp of their history reveals itself as the
merest academic platitude, involving his imagination not at
all, the extent of his immersion in French life impresses one
finally as the height of artificiality, and, even, of presumption.
The most curious thing about the passion with which he has
embraced the Continent is that it seems to be nothing more
or less than a means of safeguarding his American simplicity.
He has placed himself in a kind of strongbox of custom, and
refuses to see anything in Paris which can't be seen through
a golden haze. He is thus protected against reality, or experience, or change, and has succeeded in placing beyond the
reach of corruption values he prefers not to examine. Even
his multitudinous French friends help him to do this, for it is
impossible, after all, to be friends with a mob: they are simply
a cloud of faces, bearing witness to romance.

Between these two extremes, the student who embraces
Home, and the student who embraces The Continent—both
embraces, as we have tried to indicate, being singularly de-

void of contact, to say nothing of love—there are far more gradations than can be suggested here. The American in Europe is everywhere confronted with the question of his identity, and this may be taken as the key to all the contradictions one encounters when attempting to discuss him. Certainly, for the student colony one finds no other common denominator—this is all, really, that they have in common, and they are distinguished from each other by the ways in which they come to terms, or fail to come to terms with their confusion. This prodigious question, at home so little recognized, seems, germ-like, to be vivified in the European air, and to grow disproportionately, displacing previous assurances, and producing tensions and bewilderments entirely unlooked for. It is not, moreover, a question which limits itself to those who are, so to speak, in traffic with ideas. It confronts everyone, finding everyone unprepared; it is a question with implications not easily escaped, and the attempt to escape can precipitate disaster. Our perfectly adapted student, for example, should his strongbox of custom break, may find himself hurled into that coterie of gold-bricks who form such a spectacular element of the Paris scene that they are often what the Parisian has in the foreground of his mind when he wonderingly mutters, *C'est vraiment les Américains.* The great majority of this group, having attempted, on more or less personal levels, to lose or disguise their antecedents, are reduced to a kind of rubble of compulsion. Having cast off all previous disciplines, they have also lost the shape which these disciplines made for them and have not succeeded in finding any other. Their rejection of the limitations of American society has not set them free to function in any other society, and their illusions, therefore, remain intact: they have yet to be corrupted by the notion that society is never anything less than a perfect labyrinth of limitations. They are charmed by the reflection that Paris is more than two thousand years old, but it escapes them that the Parisian has been in the making just about that long, and that one does not, therefore, become Parisian by virtue of a Paris address. This little band of bohemians, as grimly singleminded as any evangelical sect, illustrate, by the very ferocity with which they disavow American attitudes, one of the most American of attributes, the inability to believe that time is real. It is this inability which makes them so romantic about the nature of society, and it is this inability which has led them into a total confusion about the nature of experience. Society, it would seem, is a flimsy structure, beneath contempt, designed by and for all the other people, and experience is nothing more than sensation—so many sensations, added up like arithmetic, give one the rich, full life. They thus lose what it was they so bravely set out to find, their own personalities, which, having been deprived of all nourishment, soon cease, in effect, to exist; and they arrive, finally, at a dangerous disrespect for the personalities of others. Though they persist in believing that their present shapelessness is freedom, it is observable that this present freedom is unable to endure either silence or privacy, and demands, for its ultimate expression, a rootless wandering among the cafés. Saint Germain des Près, the heart of the American colony, so far from having absorbed the American student, has been itself transformed, on spring, summer, and fall nights, into a replica, very nearly, of Times Square.

But if this were all one found in the American student colony, one would hardly have the heart to discuss it. If the American found in Europe only confusion, it would obviously be infinitely wiser for him to remain at home. Hidden, however, in the heart of the confusion he encounters here is that which he came so blindly seeking: the terms on which he is related to his country, and to the world. This, which has so grandiose and general a ring, is, in fact, most personal—the American confusion seeming to be based on the very nearly unconscious assumption that it is possible to consider the person apart from all the forces which have produced him. This assumption, however, is itself based on nothing less than our history, which is the history of the total, and willing, alienation of entire peoples from their forebears. What is overwhelmingly clear, it seems, to everyone but ourselves is that this history has created an entirely unprecedented people, with a unique and individual past. It is, indeed, this past which has thrust upon us our present, so troubling role. It is the past lived on the American continent, as against that other past, irrecoverable now on the shores of Europe, which must sustain us in the present. The truth about that past is not that it is too brief, or too superficial, but only that we, having turned our faces so resolutely away from it, have never demanded from it what it has to give. It is this demand which the American student in Paris is forced, at length, to make, for he has otherwise no identity, no reason for being here, nothing to sustain him here. From the vantage point of Europe he discovers his own country. And this is a discovery which not only brings to an end the alienation of the American from himself, but which also makes clear to him, for the first time, the extent of his involvement in the life of Europe.

Equal in Paris

On the 19th of December, in 1949, when I had been living in Paris for a little over a year, I was arrested as a receiver of stolen goods and spent eight days in prison. My arrest came about through an American tourist whom I had met twice in New York, who had been given my name and address and told to look me up. I was then living on the top floor of a ludicrously grim hotel on the rue du Bac, one of those enormous dark, cold, and hideous establishments in which Paris abounds that seem to breathe forth, in their airless, humid, stone-cold halls, the weak light, scurrying chambermaids, and creaking stairs, an odor of gentility long long dead. The place was run by an ancient Frenchman dressed in an elegant black suit which was green with age, who cannot properly be described as bewildered or even as being in a state of shock, since he had really stopped breathing around 1910. There he sat at his desk in the weirdly lit, fantastically furnished lobby, day in and day out, greeting each one of his extremely impoverished and *louche* lodgers with a stately inclination of the head that he had no doubt been taught in some impossibly remote time was the proper way for a propriétaire to greet his guests. If it had not been for his daughter, an extremely hardheaded tricoteuse—the inclination of her head was chilling and abrupt, like the downbeat of an ax—the hotel would certainly have gone bankrupt long before. It was said that this old man had not gone farther than the door of his hotel for thirty years, which was not at all difficult to believe. He looked as though the daylight would have killed him.

I did not, of course, spend much of my time in this palace. The moment I began living in French hotels I understood the necessity of French cafés. This made it rather difficult to look me up, for as soon as I was out of bed I hopefully took notebook and fountain pen off to the upstairs room of the Flore, where I consumed rather a lot of coffee and, as evening approached, rather a lot of alcohol, but did not get much writing done. But one night, in one of the cafés of St. Germain des Près, I was discovered by this New Yorker and only because we found ourselves in Paris we immediately established the illusion that we had been fast friends back in the good old U.S.A. This illusion proved itself too thin to support an evening's drinking, but by that time it was too late. I had committed myself to getting him a room in my hotel the next day, for he was living in one of the nest of hotels near the Gare St. Lazare, where, he said, the *propriétaire* was a thief, his wife a repressed nymphomaniac, the chambermaids "pigs," and the rent a crime. Americans are always talking this way about the French and so it did not occur to me that he meant what he said or that he would take into his own hands the means of avenging himself on the French Republic. It did not occur to me, either, that the means which he did take could possibly have brought about such dire results, results which were not less dire for being also comic-opera.

It came as the last of a series of disasters which had perhaps been made inevitable by the fact that I had come to
Paris originally with a little over forty dollars in my pockets,
nothing in the bank, and no grasp whatever of the French
language. It developed, shortly, that I had no grasp of the
French character either. I considered the French an ancient,
intelligent, and cultured race, which indeed they are. I did
not know, however, that ancient glories imply, at least in the
middle of the present century, present fatigue and, quite
probably, paranoia; that there is a limit to the role of the intelligence in human affairs; and that no people come into
possession of a culture without having paid a heavy price for
it. This price they cannot, of course, assess, but it is revealed
in their personalities and in their institutions. The very word
"institutions," from my side of the ocean, where, it seemed
to me, we suffered so cruelly from the lack of them, had a
pleasant ring, as of safety and order and common sense; one
had to come into contact with these institutions in order
to understand that they were also outmoded, exasperating,
completely impersonal, and very often cruel. Similarly, the
personality which had seemed from a distance to be so large
and free had to be dealt with before one could see that, if
it was large, it was also inflexible and, for the foreigner, full
of strange, high, dusty rooms which could not be inhabited.
One had, in short, to come into contact with an alien culture
in order to understand that a culture was not a community
basket-weaving project, nor yet an act of God; was something
neither desirable nor undesirable in itself, being inevitable,
being nothing more or less than the recorded and visible effects on a body of people of the vicissitudes with which they
had been forced to deal. And their great men are revealed

as simply another of these vicissitudes, even if, quite against their will, the brief battle of their great men with them has left them richer.

When my American friend left his hotel to move to mine, he took with him, out of pique, a bedsheet belonging to the hotel and put it in his suitcase. When he arrived at my hotel I borrowed the sheet, since my own were filthy and the chambermaid showed no sign of bringing me any clean ones, and put it on my bed. The sheets belonging to *my* hotel I put out in the hall, congratulating myself on having thus forced on the attention of the Grand Hôtel du Bac the unpleasant state of its linen. Thereafter, since, as it turned out, we kept very different hours—I got up at noon, when, as I gathered by meeting him on the stairs one day, he was only just getting in—my new-found friend and I saw very little of each other.

On the evening of the 19th I was sitting thinking melancholy thoughts about Christmas and staring at the walls of my room. I imagine that I had sold something or that someone had sent me a Christmas present, for I remember that I had a little money. In those days in Paris, though I floated, so to speak, on a sea of acquaintances, I knew almost no one. Many people were eliminated from my orbit by virtue of the fact that they had more money than I did, which placed me, in my own eyes, in the humiliating role of a free-loader; and other people were eliminated by virtue of the fact that they enjoyed their poverty, shrilly insisting that this wretched round of hotel rooms, bad food, humiliating concierges, and unpaid bills was the Great Adventure. It couldn't, however, for me, end soon enough, this Great Adventure; there was a real question in my mind as to which would end soonest, the Great Adventure or me. This meant, however, that there were many evenings when I sat in my room, knowing that I couldn't work there, and not knowing what to do, or whom to see. On this particular evening I went down and knocked on the American's door.

There were two Frenchmen standing in the room, who immediately introduced themselves to me as policemen; which did not worry me. I had got used to policemen in Paris bobbing up at the most improbable times and places, asking to see one's carte *d'identité*. These policemen, however, showed very little interest in my papers. They were looking for something else. I could not imagine what this would be and, since I knew I certainly didn't have it, I scarcely followed the conversation they were having with my friend. I gathered that they were looking for some kind of gangster and since I wasn't a gangster and knew that gangsterism was not, insofar as he had one, my friend's style, I was sure that the two policemen would presently bow and say *Merci, messieurs,* and leave. For by this time, I remember very clearly, I was dying to have a drink and go to dinner.

I did not have a drink or go to dinner for many days after this, and when I did my outraged stomach promptly heaved everything up again. For now one of the policemen began to exhibit the most vivid interest in me and asked, very politely, if he might see my room. To which we mounted, making, I remember, the most civilized small talk on the way and even continuing it for some moments after we were in the room in which there was certainly nothing to be seen but the familiar poverty and disorder of that precarious group of people of whatever age, race, country, calling, or intention which Paris recognizes as *les étudiants* and sometimes, more ironically and precisely, as *les nonconformistes.* Then he moved to my

bed, and in a terrible flash, not quite an instant before he
lifted the bedspread, I understood what he was looking for.
We looked at the sheet, on which I read, for the first time,
lettered in the most brilliant scarlet I have ever seen, the
name of the hotel from which it had been stolen. It was the
first time the word *stolen* entered my mind. I had certainly
seen the hotel monogram the day I put the sheet on the
bed. It had simply meant nothing to me. In New York I had
seen hotel monograms on everything from silver to soap and
towels. Taking things from New York hotels was practically
a custom, though, I suddenly realized, I had never known
anyone to take a *sheet.* Sadly, and without a word to me, the
inspector took the sheet from the bed, folded it under his
arm, and we started back downstairs. I understood that I was
under arrest.

And so we passed through the lobby, four of us, two of
us very clearly criminal, under the eyes of the old man and
his daughter, neither of whom said a word, into the streets
where a light rain was falling. And I asked, in French, "But is
this very serious?"

For I was thinking, it is, after all, only a sheet, not even new.

"No," said one of them. "It's not serious."

"It's nothing at all," said the other.

I took this to mean that we would receive a reprimand at
the police station and be allowed to go to dinner. Later on I
concluded that they were not being hypocritical or even trying to comfort us. They meant exactly what they said. It was
only that they spoke another language.

In Paris everything is very slow. Also, when dealing with
the bureaucracy, the man you are talking to is never the man
you have to see. The man you have to see has just gone off to

Belgium, or is busy with his family, or has just discovered that he is a cuckold; he will be in next Tuesday at three o'clock, or sometime in the course of the afternoon, or possibly tomorrow, or, possibly, in the next five minutes. But if he is coming in the next five minutes he will be far too busy to be able to see you today. So that I suppose I was not really astonished to learn at the commissariat that nothing could possibly be done about us before The Man arrived in the morning. But no, we could not go off and have dinner and come back in the morning. Of course he knew that we *would* come back—that was not the question. Indeed, there was no question: we would simply have to stay there for the night. We were placed in a cell which rather resembled a chicken coop. It was now about seven in the evening and I relinquished the thought of dinner and began to think of lunch.

I discouraged the chatter of my New York friend and this left me alone with my thoughts. I was beginning to be frightened and I bent all my energies, therefore, to keeping my panic under control. I began to realize that I was in a country I knew nothing about, in the hands of a people I did not understand at all. In a similar situation in New York I would have had some idea of what to do because I would have had some idea of what to expect. I am not speaking now of legality which, like most of the poor, I had never for an instant trusted, but of the temperament of the people with whom I had to deal. I had become very accomplished in New York at guessing and, therefore, to a limited extent manipulating to my advantage the reactions of the white world. But this was not New York. None of my old weapons could serve me here. I did not know what they saw when they looked at me. I knew very well what Americans saw when they looked at me and this allowed me to play endless and sinister variations on the role which they had assigned me; since I knew that it was, for them, of the utmost importance that they never be confronted with what, in their own personalities, made this role so necessary and gratifying to them, I knew that they could never call my hand or, indeed, afford to know what I was doing; so that I moved into every crucial situation with the deadly and rather desperate advantages of bitterly accumulated perception, of pride and contempt. This is an awful sword and shield to carry through the world, and the discovery that, in the game I was playing, I did myself a violence of which the world, at its most ferocious, would scarcely have been capable, was what had driven me out of New York. It was a strange feeling, in this situation, after a year in Paris, to discover that my weapons would never again serve me as they had.

It was quite clear to me that the Frenchmen in whose hands I found myself were no better or worse than their American counterparts. Certainly their uniforms frightened me quite as much, and their impersonality, and the threat, always very keenly felt by the poor, of violence, was as present in that commissariat as it had ever been for me in any police station. And I had seen, for example, what Paris policemen could do to Arab peanut vendors. The only difference here was that I did not understand these people, did not know what techniques their cruelty took, did not know enough about their personalities to see danger coming, to ward it off, did not know on what ground to meet it. That evening in the commissariat I was not a despised black man. They would simply have laughed at me if I had behaved like one. For them, I was an American. And here it was they who had the advantage, for that word, *Américain,* gave them some idea, far from inaccurate, of what to expect from me. In order to corroborate none of their ironical expectations I said nothing and did nothing—which was not the way any Frenchman, white or black, would have reacted. The question thrusting up from the bottom of my mind was not *what* I was, but *who.* And this question, since a *what* can get by with skill but a *who* demands resources, was my first real intimation of what humility must mean.

In the morning it was still raining. Between nine and ten o'clock a black Citroën took us off to the Ile de la Cité, to the great, gray Préfecture. I realize now that the questions I put to the various policemen who escorted us were always answered in such a way as to corroborate what I wished to hear. This was not out of politeness, but simply out of in-difference—or, possibly, an ironical pity—since each of the policemen knew very well that nothing would speed or halt the machine in which I had become entangled. They knew I did not know this and there was certainly no point in their telling me. In one way or another I would certainly come out at the other side—for they also knew that being found with a stolen bedsheet in one's possession was not a crime pun-ishable by the guillotine. (They had the advantage over me there, too, for there were certainly moments later on when I was not so sure.) If I did *not* come out at the other side— well, that was just too bad. So, to my question, put while we were in the Citroën—"Will it be over today?"—I received a *"Oui, bien sûr."* He was not lying. As it turned out, the *procès-verbal* was over that day. Trying to be realistic, I dis-missed, in the Citroën, all thoughts of lunch and pushed my mind ahead to dinner.

At the Préfecture we were first placed in a tiny cell, in which it was almost impossible either to sit or to lie down. After a couple of hours of this we were taken down to an office, where, for the first time, I encountered the owner of the bedsheet and where the *procès-verbal* took place. This was simply an interrogation, quite chillingly clipped and efficient (so that there was, shortly, no doubt in one's own mind that one *should* be treated as a criminal), which was recorded by a secretary. When it was over, this report was given to us to sign. One had, of course, no choice but to sign it, even though my mastery of written French was very far from certain. We were being held, according to the law in France, incommunicado, and all my angry demands to be allowed to speak to my embassy or to see a lawyer met with a stony "*Oui, oui. Plus tard.*" The *procès-verbal* over, we were taken back to the cell, before which, shortly, passed the owner of the bedsheet. He said he hoped we had slept well, gave a vindictive wink, and disappeared.

By this time there was only one thing clear: that we had no way of controlling the sequence of events and could not possibly guess what this sequence would be. It seemed to me, since what I regarded as the high point—the *procès-verbal*—had been passed and since the hotel-keeper was once again in possession of his sheet, that we might reasonably expect to be released from police custody in a matter of hours. We had been detained now for what would soon be twenty-four hours, during which time I had learned only that the official charge against me was *receleur.* My mental shifting, between lunch and dinner, to say nothing of the physical lack of either of these delights, was beginning to make me dizzy. The steady chatter of my friend from New York, who was

determined to keep my spirits up, made me feel murderous; I was praying that some power would release us from
this freezing pile of stone before the impulse became the act.
And I was beginning to wonder what was happening in that
beautiful city, Paris, which lived outside these walls. I wondered how long it would take before anyone casually asked,
"But where's Jimmy? He hasn't been around"—and realized,
knowing the people I knew, that it would take several days.

Quite late in the afternoon we were taken from our cells;
handcuffed, each to a separate officer; led through a maze of
steps and corridors to the top of the building; fingerprinted;
photographed. As in movies I had seen, I was placed against
a wall, facing an old-fashioned camera, behind which stood
one of the most completely cruel and indifferent faces I had
ever seen, while someone next to me and, therefore, just outside my line of vision, read off in a voice from which all human feeling, even feeling of the most base description, had
long since fled, what must be called my public characteristics—which, at that time and in that place, seemed anything
but that. He might have been roaring to the hostile world se-
crets which I could barely, in the privacy of midnight, utter to
myself. But he was only reading off my height, my features,
my approximate weight, my color—that color which, in the
United States, had often, odd as it may sound, been my salvation—the color of my hair, my age, my nationality. A light
then flashed, the photographer and I staring at each other as
though there was murder in our hearts, and then it was over.
Handcuffed again, I was led downstairs to the bottom of the
building, into a great enclosed shed in which had been gathered the very scrapings off the Paris streets. Old, old men,
so ruined and old that life in them seemed really to prove

the miracle of the quickening power of the Holy Ghost—for clearly their life was no longer their affair, it was no longer even their burden, they were simply the clay which had once been touched. And men not so old, with faces the color of lead and the consistency of oatmeal, eyes that made me think of stale *café-au-lait* spiked with arsenic, bodies which could take in food and water—any food and water—and pass it out, but which could not do anything more, except possibly, at midnight, along the riverbank where rats scurried, rape. And young men, harder and crueler than the Paris stones, older by far than I, their chronological senior by some five to seven years. And North Africans, old and young, who seemed the only living people in this place because they yet retained the grace to be bewildered. But they were not bewildered by being in this shed: they were simply bewildered because they were no longer in North Africa. There was a great hole in the center of this shed, which was the common toilet. Near it, though it was impossible to get very far from it, stood an old man with white hair, eating a piece of camembert. It was at this point, probably, that thought, for me, stopped, that physiology, if one may say so, took over. I found myself incapable of saying a word, not because I was afraid I would cry but because I was afraid I would vomit. And I did not think any longer of the city of Paris but my mind flew back to that home from which I had fled. I was sure that I would never see it any more. And it must have seemed to me that my flight from home was the cruelest trick I had ever played on myself, since it had led me here, down to a lower point than any I could ever in my life have imagined—lower, far, than anything I had seen in that Harlem which I had so hated and so loved, the escape from which had soon become the greatest direction of my life. After we had been here an hour or so a functionary came and opened the door and called out our names. And I was sure that *this* was my release. But I was handcuffed again and led out of the Préfecture into the streets—it was dark now, it was still raining—and before the steps of the Préfecture stood the great police wagon, doors facing me, wide open. The handcuffs were taken off, I entered the wagon, which was peculiarly constructed. It was divided by a narrow aisle, and on each side of the aisle was a series of narrow doors. These doors opened on a narrow cubicle, beyond which was a door which opened onto another narrow cubicle: three or four cubicles, each private, with a locking door. I was placed in one of them; I remember there was a small vent just above my head which let in a little light. The door of my cubicle was locked from the outside. I had no idea where this wagon was taking me and, as it began to move, I began to cry. I suppose I cried all the way to prison, the prison called Fresnes, which is twelve kilometers outside of Paris.

For reasons I have no way at all of understanding, prisoners whose last initial is A, B, or C are always sent to Fresnes; everybody else is sent to a prison called, rather cynically it seems to me, La Santé. I will, obviously, never be allowed to enter La Santé, but I was told by people who certainly seemed to know that it was infinitely more unbearable than Fresnes. This arouses in me, until today, a positive storm of curiosity concerning what I promptly began to think of as The Other Prison. My colleague in crime, occurring lower in the alphabet, had been sent there and I confess that the minute he was gone I missed him. I missed him because he was not French and because he was the only person in the world who knew that the story I told was true.

For, once locked in, divested of shoelaces, belt, watch, money, papers, nailfile, in a freezing cell in which both the window and the toilet were broken, with six other adventures, the story I told of *l'affaire du drap de lit* elicited only the wildest amusement or the most suspicious disbelief. Among the people who shared my cell the first three days no one, it is true, had been arrested for anything much more serious—or, at least, not serious in my eyes. I remember that there was a boy who had stolen a knitted sweater from a *monoprix*, who would probably, it was agreed, receive a six-month sentence. There was an older man there who had been arrested for some kind of petty larceny. There were two North Africans, vivid, brutish, and beautiful, who alternated between gaiety and fury, not at the fact of their arrest but at the state of the cell. None poured as much emotional energy into the fact of their arrest as I did; they took it, as I would have liked to take it, as simply another unlucky happening in a very dirty world. For, though I had grown accustomed to thinking of myself as looking upon the world with a hard, penetrating eye, the truth was that they were far more realistic about the world than I, and more nearly right about it. The gap between us, which only a gesture I made could have bridged, grew steadily, during thirty-six hours, wider. I could not make any gesture simply because they frightened me. I was unable to accept my imprisonment as a fact, even as a temporary fact. I could not, even for a moment, accept my present companions as *my* companions. And they, of course, felt this and put it down, with perfect justice, to the fact that I was an American.

There was nothing to do all day long. It appeared that we would one day come to trial but no one knew when. We were awakened at seven-thirty by a rapping on what I believe is called the Judas, that small opening in the door of the cell which allows the guards to survey the prisoners. At this rapping we rose from the floor—we slept on straw pallets and each of us was covered with one thin blanket—and moved to the door of the cell. We peered through the opening into the center of the prison, which was, as I remember, three tiers high, all gray stone and gunmetal steel, precisely that prison I had seen in movies, except that, in the movies, I had not known that it was cold in prison. I had not known that when one's shoelaces and belt have been removed one is, in the strangest way, demoralized. The necessity of shuffling and the necessity of holding up one's trousers with one hand turn one into a rag doll. And the movies fail, of course, to give one any idea of what prison food is like. Along the corridor, at seven-thirty, came three men, each pushing before him a great garbage can, mounted on wheels. In the garbage can of the first was the bread—this was passed to one through the small opening in the door. In the can of the second was the coffee. In the can of the third was what was always called *la soupe,* a pallid paste of potatoes which had certainly been bubbling on the back of the prison stove long before that first, so momentous revolution. Naturally, it was cold by this time and, starving as I was, I could not eat it. I drank the coffee—which was not coffee—because it was hot, and spent the rest of the day, huddled in my blanket, munching on the bread. It was not the French bread one bought in bakeries. In the evening the same procession returned. At ten-thirty the lights went out. I had a recurring dream, each night, a nightmare which always involved my mother's fried chicken. At the moment I was about to eat it came the rapping at the door. Silence is really all I remember of those first three days, silence and the color gray.

I am not sure now whether it was on the third or the fourth day that I was taken to trial for the first time. The days had nothing, obviously, to distinguish them from one another. I remember that I was very much aware that Christmas Day was approaching and I wondered if I was really going to spend Christmas Day in prison. And I remember that the first trial came the day before Christmas Eve.

On the morning of the first trial I was awakened by hearing my name called. I was told, hanging in a kind of void between my mother's fried chicken and the cold prison floor, "*Vous préparez. Vous êtes extrait*"—which simply terrified me, since I did not know what interpretation to put on the word "*extrait*," and since my cellmates had been amusing themselves with me by telling terrible stories about the inefficiency of French prisons, an inefficiency so extreme that it had often happened that someone who was supposed to be taken out and tried found himself on the wrong line and was guillotined instead. The best way of putting my reaction to this is to say that, though I knew they were teasing me, it was simply not possible for me to totally *dis*believe them. As far as I was concerned, once in the hands of the law in France, anything could happen. I shuffled along with the others who were *extrait* to the center of the prison, trying, rather, to linger in the office, which seemed the only warm spot in the whole world, and found myself again in that dreadful wagon, and was carried again to the Ile de la Cité, this time to the Palais de Justice. The entire day, except for ten minutes, was spent in one of the cells, first waiting to be tried, then waiting to be taken back to prison.

For I was *not* tried that day. By and by I was handcuffed and led through the halls, upstairs to the courtroom where I found my New York friend. We were placed together, both stage-whisperingly certain that this was the end of our ordeal. Nevertheless, while I waited for our case to be called, my eyes searched the courtroom, looking for a face I knew, hoping, anyway, that there was someone there who knew *me,* who would carry to someone outside the news that I was in trouble. But there was no one I knew there and I had had time to realize that there was probably only one man in Paris who could help me, an American patent attorney for whom I had worked as an office boy. He could have helped me because he had a quite solid position and some prestige and would have testified that, while working for him, I had handled large sums of money regularly, which made it rather unlikely that I would stoop to trafficking in bedsheets. However, he was somewhere in Paris, probably at this very moment enjoying a snack and a glass of wine and as far as the possibility of reaching him was concerned, he might as well have been on Mars. I tried to watch the proceedings and to make my mind a blank. But the proceedings were not reassuring. The boy, for example, who had stolen the sweater *did* receive a six-month sentence. It seemed to me that all the sentences meted out that day were excessive; though, again, it seemed that all the people who were sentenced that day had made, or clearly were going to make, crime their career. This seemed to be the opinion of the judge, who scarcely looked at the prisoners or listened to them; it seemed to be the opinion of the prisoners, who scarcely bothered to speak in their own behalf; it seemed to be the opinion of the lawyers, state lawyers for the most part, who were defending them. The great impulse of the courtroom seemed to be to put these people where they could not be seen—and not because they were offended at the crimes, unless, indeed, they were offended that the crimes were so petty, but because they did not wish to know that their society could be counted on to produce, probably in greater and greater numbers, a whole body of people for whom crime was the only possible career. Any society inevitably produces its criminals, but a society at once rigid and unstable can do nothing whatever to alleviate the poverty of its lowest members, cannot present to the hypothetical young man at the crucial moment that so-well-advertised right path. And the fact, perhaps, that the French are the earth's least sentimental people and must also be numbered among the most proud aggravates the plight of their lowest, youngest, and unluckiest members, for it means that the idea of rehabilitation is scarcely real to them. I confess that this attitude on their part raises in me sentiments of exasperation, admiration, and despair, revealing as it does, in both the best and the worst sense, their renowned and spectacular hard-headedness.

Finally our case was called and we rose. We gave our names. At the point that it developed that we were American the proceedings ceased, a hurried consultation took place between the judge and what I took to be several lawyers. Someone called out for an interpreter. The arresting officer had forgotten to mention our nationalities and there was, therefore, no interpreter in the court. Even if our French had been better than it was we would not have been allowed to stand trial without an interpreter. Before I clearly understood what was happening, I was handcuffed again and led out of the courtroom. The trial had been set back for the 27th of December.

I have sometimes wondered if I would *ever* have got out of prison if it had not been for the older man who had been arrested for the mysterious petty larceny. He was acquitted that day and when he returned to the cell—for he could not be released until morning—he found me sitting numbly on the floor, having just been prevented, by the sight of a man, all blood, being carried back to *his* cell on a stretcher, from seizing the bars and screaming until they let me out. The sight of the man on the stretcher proved, however, that screaming would not do much for me. The petty-larceny man went around asking if he could do anything in the world outside for those he was leaving behind. When he came to me I, at first, responded, "No, nothing"—for I suppose I had by now retreated into the attitude, the earliest I remember, that of my father, which was simply (since I had lost his God) that nothing could help me. And I suppose I will remember with gratitude until I die the fact that the man now insisted: "*Mais, êtes-vous sûr?*" Then it swept over me that he was going *outside* and he instantly became my first contact since the Lord alone knew how long with the outside world. At the same time, I remember, I did not really believe that he would help me. There was no reason why he should. But I gave him the phone number of my attorney friend and my own name.

So, in the middle of the next day, Christmas Eve, I shuffled downstairs again, to meet my visitor. He looked extremely well fed and sane and clean. He told me I had nothing to worry about any more. Only not even he could do anything to make the mill of justice grind any faster. He would, however, send me a lawyer of his acquaintance who would defend me on the 27th, and he would himself, along with several other people, appear as a character witness. He gave me a package of Lucky Strikes (which the turnkey took from me on the way upstairs) and said that, though it was doubtful that there would be any celebration in the prison, he would see to it that I got a fine Christmas dinner when I got out. And this, somehow, seemed very funny. I remember being astonished at the discovery that I was actually laughing. I was, too, I imagine, also rather disappointed that my hair had not turned white, that my face was clearly not going to bear any marks of tragedy, disappointed at bottom, no doubt, to realize, facing him in that room, that far worse things had happened to most people and that, indeed, to paraphrase my mother, if this was the worst thing that ever happened to me I could consider myself among the luckiest people ever to be born. He injected—my visitor—into my solitary nightmare common sense, the world, and the hint of blacker things to come.

The next day, Christmas, unable to endure my cell, and feeling that, after all, the day demanded a gesture, I asked to be allowed to go to Mass, hoping to hear some music. But I found myself, for a freezing hour and a half, locked in exactly the same kind of cubicle as in the wagon which had first brought me to prison, peering through a slot placed at the level of the eye at an old Frenchman, hatted, overcoated, muffled, and gloved, preaching in this language which I did not understand, to this row of wooden boxes, the story of Jesus Christ's love for men.

The next day, the 26th, I spent learning a peculiar kind of game, played with match-sticks, with my cellmates. For, since I no longer felt that I would stay in this cell forever, I was beginning to be able to make peace with it for a time. On the 27th I went again to trial and, as had been predicted, the case against us was dismissed. The story of the *drap de lit,* finally told, caused great merriment in the courtroom, whereupon my friend decided that the French were "great." I was chilled by their merriment, even though it was meant to warm me. It could only remind me of the laughter I had often heard at home, laughter which I had sometimes deliberately elicited. This laughter is the laughter of those who consider themselves to be at a safe remove from all the wretched, for whom the pain of the living is not real. I had heard it so often in my native land that I had resolved to find a place where I would never hear it any more. In some deep, black, stony, and liberating way, my life, in my own eyes, began during that first year in Paris, when it was borne in on me that this laughter is universal and never can be stilled.

Stranger in the Village

From all available evidence no black man had ever set foot in this tiny Swiss village before I came. I was told before arriving that I would probably be a "sight" for the village; I took this to mean that people of my complexion were rarely seen in Switzerland, and also that city people are always something of a "sight" outside of the city. It did not occur to me—possibly because I am an American—that there could be people anywhere who had never seen a Negro.

It is a fact that cannot be explained on the basis of the inaccessibility of the village. The village is very high, but it is only four hours from Milan and three hours from Lausanne. It is true that it is virtually unknown. Few people making plans for a holiday would elect to come here. On the other hand, the villagers are able, presumably, to come and go as they please—which they do: to another town at the foot of the mountain, with a population of approximately five thousand, the nearest place to see a movie or go to the bank, In the village there is no movie house, no bank, no library, no theater; very few radios, one jeep, one station wagon; and, at the moment, one typewriter, mine, an invention which the woman next door to me here had never seen. There are

about six hundred people living here, all Catholic—I conclude this from the fact that the Catholic church is open all
year round, whereas the Protestant chapel, set off on a hill a
little removed from the village, is open only in the summertime when the tourists arrive. There are four or five hotels, all
closed now, and four or five *bistros,* of which, however, only
two do any business during the winter. These two do not do a
great deal, for life in the village seems to end around nine or
ten o'clock. There are a few stores, butcher, baker, *épicerie,* a
hardware store, and a money-changer—who cannot change
travelers' checks, but must send them down to the bank, an
operation which takes two or three days. There is something
called the *Ballet Haus,* closed in the winter and used for God
knows what, certainly not ballet, during the summer. There
seems to be only one schoolhouse in the village, and this for
the quite young children; I suppose this to mean that their
older brothers and sisters at some point descend from these
mountains in order to complete their education—possibly,
again, to the town just below. The landscape is absolutely for-
bidding, mountains towering on all four sides, ice and snow
as far as the eye can reach. In this white wilderness, men
and women and children move all day, carrying washing,
wood, buckets of milk or water, sometimes skiing on Sunday afternoons. All week long boys and young men are to be
seen shoveling snow off the rooftops, or dragging wood down
from the forest in sleds.

The village's only real attraction, which explains the tourist
season, is the hot spring water. A disquietingly high propor-
tion of these tourists are cripples, or semicripples, who come
year after year—from other parts of Switzerland, usually—to
take the waters. This lends the village, at the height of the

season, a rather terrifying air of sanctity, as though it were a lesser Lourdes. There is often something beautiful, there is always something awful, in the spectacle of a person who has lost one of his faculties, a faculty he never questioned until it was gone, and who struggles to recover it. Yet people remain people, on crutches or indeed on deathbeds; and wherever I passed, the first summer I was here, among the native villagers or among the lame, a wind passed with me—of astonishment, curiosity, amusement, and outrage. That first summer I stayed two weeks and never intended to return. But I did return in the winter, to work; the village offers, obviously, no distractions whatever and has the further advantage of being extremely cheap. Now it is winter again, a year later, and I am here again. Everyone in the village knows my name, though they scarcely ever use it, knows that I come from America— though, this, apparently, they will never really believe: black men come from Africa—and everyone knows that I am the friend of the son of a woman who was born here, and that I am staying in their chalet. But I remain as much a stranger today as I was the first day I arrived, and the children shout *Neger! Neger!* as I walk along the streets.

It must be admitted that in the beginning I was far too shocked to have any real reaction. In so far as I reacted at all, I reacted by trying to be pleasant—it being a great part of the American Negro's education (long before he goes to school) that he must make people "like" him. This smile-and-the-world-smiles-with-you routine worked about as well in this situation as it had in the situation for which it was designed, which is to say that it did not work at all. No one, after all, can be liked whose human weight and complexity cannot be, or has not been, admitted. My smile was simply another unheard-of phenomenon which allowed them to see my teeth—they did not, really, see my smile and I began to think that, should I take to snarling, no one would notice any difference. All of the physical characteristics of the Negro which had caused me, in America, a very different and almost forgotten pain were nothing less than miraculous—or infernal—in the eyes of the village people. Some thought my hair was the color of tar, that it had the texture of wire, or the texture of cotton. It was jocularly suggested that I might let it all grow long and make myself a winter coat. If I sat in the sun for more than five minutes some daring creature was certain to come along and gingerly put his fingers on my hair, as though he were afraid of an electric shock, or put his hand on my hand, astonished that the color did not rub off. In all of this, in which it must be conceded there was the charm of genuine wonder and in which there was certainly no element of intentional unkindness, there was yet no suggestion that I was human: I was simply a living wonder.

I knew that they did not mean to be unkind, and I know it now; it is necessary, nevertheless, for me to repeat this to myself each time that I walk out of the chalet. The children who shout *Neger!* have no way of knowing the echoes this sound raises in me. They are brimming with good humor and the more daring swell with pride when I stop to speak with them. Just the same, there are days when I cannot pause and smile, when I have no heart to play with them; when, indeed, I mutter sourly to myself, exactly as I muttered on the streets of a city these children have never seen, when I was no bigger than these children are now: *Your* mother *was a nigger.* Joyce is right about history being a nightmare—but it may be the nightmare from which no one *can* awaken. People are trapped in history and history is trapped in them.

There is a custom in the village—I am told it is repeated in many villages—of "buying" African natives for the purpose of converting them to Christianity. There stands in the church all year round a small box with a slot for money, decorated with a black figurine, and into this box the villagers drop their francs. During the *carnaval* which precedes Lent, two village children have their faces blackened—out of which bloodless darkness their blue eyes shine like ice—and fantastic horse-hair wigs are placed on their blond heads; thus disguised, they solicit among the villagers for money for the missionaries in Africa. Between the box in the church and the blackened children, the village "bought" last year six or eight African natives. This was reported to me with pride by the wife of one of the *bistro* owners and I was careful to express astonishment and pleasure at the solicitude shown by the village for the souls of black folk. The *bistro* owner's wife beamed with a pleasure far more genuine than my own and seemed to feel that I might now breathe more easily concerning the souls of at least six of my kinsmen.

I tried not to think of these so lately baptized kinsmen, of the price paid for them, or the peculiar price they themselves would pay, and said nothing about my father, who having taken his own conversion too literally never, at bottom, forgave the white world (which he described as heathen) for having saddled him with a Christ in whom, to judge at least from their treatment of him, they themselves no longer believed. I thought of white men arriving for the first time in an African village, strangers there, as I am a stranger here, and tried to imagine the astounded populace touching their hair and marveling at the color of their skin. But there is a great difference between being the first white man to be seen by Africans and being the first black man to be seen by whites. The white man takes the astonishment as tribute, for he arrives to conquer and to convert the natives, whose inferiority in relation to himself is not even to be questioned; whereas I, without a thought of conquest, find myself among a people whose culture controls me, has even, in a sense, created me, people who have cost me more in anguish and rage than they will ever know, who yet do not even know of my existence. The astonishment with which I might have greeted them, should they have stumbled into my African village a few hundred years ago, might have rejoiced their hearts. But the astonishment with which they greet me today can only poison mine.

And this is so despite everything I may do to feel differently, despite my friendly conversations with the *bistro* owner's wife, despite their three-year-old son who has at last become my friend, despite the *saluts* and *bonsoirs* which I exchange with people as I walk, despite the fact that I know that no individual can be taken to task for what history is doing, or has done. I say that the culture of these people controls me—but they can scarcely be held responsible for European culture. America comes out of Europe, but these people have never seen America, nor have most of them seen more of Europe than the hamlet at the foot of their mountain. Yet they move with an authority which I shall never have; and they regard me, quite rightly, not only as a stranger in their village but as a suspect latecomer, bearing no credentials, to everything they have—however unconsciously—inherited.

For this village, even were it incomparably more remote and incredibly more primitive, is the West, the West onto which I have been so strangely grafted. These people cannot be, from the point of view of power, strangers anywhere in the world; they have made the modern world, in effect, even if they do not know it. The most illiterate among them is related, in a way that I am not, to Dante, Shakespeare, Michelangelo, Aeschylus, Da Vinci, Rembrandt, and Racine; the cathedral at Chartres says something to them which it cannot say to me, as indeed would New York's Empire State Building, should anyone here ever see it. Out of their hymns and dances come Beethoven and Bach. Go back a few centuries and they are in their full glory—but I am in Africa, watching the conquerors arrive.

The rage of the disesteemed is personally fruitless, but it is also absolutely inevitable; this rage, so generally discounted, so little understood even among the people whose daily bread it is, is one of the things that makes history. Rage can only with difficulty, and never entirely, be brought under the domination of the intelligence and is therefore not susceptible to any arguments whatever. This is a fact which ordinary representatives of the *Herrenvolk*, having never felt this rage and being unable to imagine it, quite fail to understand. Also, rage cannot be hidden, it can only be dissembled. This dissembling deludes the thoughtless, and strengthens rage and adds, to rage, contempt. There are, no doubt, as many ways of coping with the resulting complex of tensions as there are black men in the world, but no black man can hope ever to be entirely liberated from this internal warfare—rage, dissembling, and contempt having inevitably accompanied his first realization of the power of white men. What is crucial here is

that, since white men represent in the black man's world so
heavy a weight, white men have for black men a reality which
is far from being reciprocal; and hence all black men have
toward all white men an attitude which is designed, really,
either to rob the white man of the jewel of his naïveté, or else
to make it cost him dear.

The black man insists, by whatever means he finds at his
disposal, that the white man cease to regard him as an ex-
otic rarity and recognize him as a human being. This is a very
charged and difficult moment, for there is a great deal of will
power involved in the white man's naïveté. Most people are
not naturally reflective any more than they are naturally mali-
cious, and the white man prefers to keep the black man at
a certain human remove because it is easier for him thus to
preserve his simplicity and avoid being called to account for
crimes committed by his forefathers, or his neighbors. He is
inescapably aware, nevertheless, that he is in a better position in the world than black men are, nor can he quite put to
death the suspicion that he is hated by black men therefore.
He does not wish to be hated, neither does he wish to change
places, and at this point in his uneasiness he can scarcely avoid
having recourse to those legends which white men have created about black men, the most usual effect of which is that
the white man finds himself enmeshed, so to speak, in his own
language which describes hell, as well as the attributes which
lead one to hell, as being as black as night.

Every legend, moreover, contains its residuum of truth,
and the root function of language is to control the universe
by describing it. It is of quite considerable significance that
black men remain, in the imagination, and in overwhelming numbers in fact, beyond the disciplines of salvation; and

this despite the fact that the West has been "buying" African natives for centuries. There is, I should hazard, an instantaneous necessity to be divorced from this so visibly unsaved stranger, in whose heart, moreover, one cannot guess what dreams of vengeance are being nourished; and, at the same time, there are few things on earth more attractive than the idea of the unspeakable liberty which is allowed the unredeemed. When, beneath the black mask, a human being begins to make himself felt one cannot escape a certain awful wonder as to what kind of human being it is. What one's imagination makes of other people is dictated, of course, by the laws of one's own personality and it is one of the ironies of black-white relations that, by means of what the white man imagines the black man to be, the black man is enabled to know who the white man is.

I have said, for example, that I am as much a stranger in this village today as I was the first summer I arrived, but this is not quite true. The villagers wonder less about the texture of my hair than they did then, and wonder rather more about me. And the fact that their wonder now exists on another level is reflected in their attitudes and in their eyes. There are the children who make those delightful, hilarious, sometimes astonishingly grave overtures of friendship in the unpredictable fashion of children; other children, having been taught that the devil is a black man, scream in genuine anguish as I approach. Some of the older women never pass without a friendly greeting, never pass, indeed, if it seems that they will be able to engage me in conversation; other women look down or look away or rather contemptuously smirk. Some of the men drink with me and suggest that I learn how to ski— partly, I gather, because they cannot imagine what I would

look like on skis—and want to know if I am married, and ask
questions about my *métier*. But some of the men have accused *le sale nègre*—behind my back—of stealing wood and
there is already in the eyes of some of them that peculiar, in-
tent, paranoiac malevolence which one sometimes surprises
in the eyes of American white men when, out walking with
their Sunday girl, they see a Negro male approach.

There is a dreadful abyss between the streets of this village and the streets of the city in which I was born, between
the children who shout *Neger!* today and those who shouted
Nigger! yesterday—the abyss is experience, the American
experience. The syllable hurled behind me today expresses,
above all, wonder: I am a stranger here. But I am not a
stranger in America and the same syllable riding on the
American air expresses the war my presence has occasioned
in the American soul.

For this village brings home to me this fact: that there was
a day, and not really a very distant day, when Americans were
scarcely Americans at all but discontented Europeans, facing
a great unconquered continent and strolling, say, into a mar-
ketplace and seeing black men for the first time. The shock
this spectacle afforded is suggested, surely, by the promptness
with which they decided that these black men were not really
men but cattle. It is true that the necessity on the part of the
settlers of the New World of reconciling their moral assumptions with the fact—and the necessity—of slavery enhanced
immensely the charm of this idea, and it is also true that this
idea expresses, with a truly American bluntness, the attitude
which to varying extents all masters have had toward all slaves.

But between all former slaves and slave-owners and the
drama which begins for Americans over three hundred years

ago at Jamestown, there are at least two differences to be observed. The American Negro slave could not suppose, for one thing, as slaves in past epochs had supposed and often done, that he would ever be able to wrest the power from his master's hands. This was a supposition which the modern era, which was to bring about such vast changes in the aims and dimensions of power, put to death; it only begins, in unprecedented fashion, and with dreadful implications, to be resurrected today. But even had this supposition persisted with undiminished force, the American Negro slave could not have used it to lend his condition dignity, for the reason that this supposition rests on another: that the slave in exile yet remains related to his past, has some means—if only in memory—of revering and sustaining the forms of his former life, is able, in short, to maintain his identity.

This was not the case with the American Negro slave. He is unique among the black men of the world in that his past was taken from him, almost literally, at one blow. One wonders what on earth the first slave found to say to the first dark child he bore. I am told that there are Haitians able to trace their ancestry back to African kings, but any American Negro wishing to go back so far will find his journey through time abruptly arrested by the signature on the bill of sale which served as the entrance paper for his ancestor. At the time— to say nothing of the circumstances—of the enslavement of the captive black man who was to become the American Negro, there was not the remotest possibility that he would ever take power from his master's hands. There was no reason to suppose that his situation would ever change, nor was there, shortly, anything to indicate that his situation had ever been different. It was his necessity, in the words of E. Franklin

Frazier, to find a "motive for living under American culture or die." The identity of the American Negro comes out of this extreme situation, and the evolution of this identity was a source of the most intolerable anxiety in the minds and the lives of his masters.

For the history of the American Negro is unique also in this: that the question of his humanity, and of his rights therefore as a human being, became a burning one for several generations of Americans, so burning a question that it ultimately became one of those used to divide the nation. It is out of this argument that the venom of the epithet *Nigger!* is derived. It is an argument which Europe has never had, and hence Europe quite sincerely fails to understand how or why the argument arose in the first place, why its effects are so frequently disastrous and always so unpredictable, why it refuses until today to be entirely settled. Europe's black possessions remained—and do remain—in Europe's colonies, at which remove they represented no threat whatever to European identity. If they posed any problem at all for the European conscience, it was a problem which remained comfortingly abstract: in effect, the black man, *as a man,* did not exist for Europe. But in America, even as a slave, he was an inescapable part of the general social fabric and no American could escape having an attitude toward him. Americans attempt until today to make an abstraction of the Negro, but the very nature of these abstractions reveals the tremendous effects the presence of the Negro has had on the American character.

When one considers the history of the Negro in America it is of the greatest importance to recognize that the moral beliefs of a person, or a people, are never really as tenuous as life—which is not moral—very often causes them to appear; these create for them a frame of reference and a necessary hope, the hope being that when life has done its worst they will be enabled to rise above themselves and to triumph over life. Life would scarcely be bearable if this hope did not exist. Again, even when the worst has been said, to betray a belief is not by any means to have put oneself beyond its power; the betrayal of a belief is not the same thing as ceasing to believe. If this were not so there would be no moral standards in the world at all. Yet one must also recognize that morality is based on ideas and that all ideas are dangerous—dangerous because ideas can only lead to action and where the action leads no man can say. And dangerous in this respect: that confronted with the impossibility of remaining faithful to one's beliefs, and the equal impossibility of becoming free of them, one can be driven to the most inhuman excesses. The ideas on which American beliefs are based are not, though Americans often seem to think so, ideas which originated in America. They came out of Europe. And the establishment of democracy on the American continent was scarcely as radical a break with the past as was the necessity, which Americans faced, of broadening this concept to include black men.

This was, literally, a hard necessity. It was impossible, for one thing, for Americans to abandon their beliefs, not only because these beliefs alone seemed able to justify the sacrifices they had endured and the blood that they had spilled, but also because these beliefs afforded them their only bulwark against a moral chaos as absolute as the physical chaos of the continent it was their destiny to conquer. But in the situation in which Americans found themselves, these beliefs threatened an idea which, whether or not one likes to think so, is the very warp and woof of the heritage of the West, the idea of white supremacy.

Americans have made themselves notorious by the shrillness and the brutality with which they have insisted on this idea, but they did not invent it; and it has escaped the world's notice that those very excesses of which Americans have been guilty imply a certain, unprecedented uneasiness over the idea's life and power, if not, indeed, the idea's validity. The idea of white supremacy rests simply on the fact that white men are the creators of civilization (the present civilization, which is the only one that matters; all previous civilizations are simply "contributions" to our own) and are therefore civilization's guardians and defenders. Thus it was impossible for Americans to accept the black man as one of themselves, for to do so was to jeopardize their status as white men. But not so to accept him was to deny his human reality, his human weight and complexity, and the strain of denying the overwhelmingly undeniable forced Americans into rationalizations so fantastic that they approached the pathological.

At the root of the American Negro problem is the necessity of the American white man to find a way of living with the Negro in order to be able to live with himself. And the history of this problem can be reduced to the means used by Americans—lynch law and law, segregation and legal acceptance, terrorization and concession—either to come to terms with this necessity, or to find a way around it, or (most usually) to find a way of doing both these things at once. The resulting spectacle, at once foolish and dreadful, led someone to make the quite accurate observation that "the Negro-in-America is a form of insanity which overtakes white men."

In this long battle, a battle by no means finished, the un-
foreseeable effects of which will be felt by many future generations, the white man's motive was the protection of his
identity; the black man was motivated by the need to establish an identity. And despite the terrorization which the Negro in America endured and endures sporadically until today,
despite the cruel and totally inescapable ambivalence of his
status in his country, the battle for his identity has long ago
been won. He is not a visitor to the West, but a citizen there,
an American; as American as the Americans who despise
him, the Americans who fear him, the Americans who love
him—the Americans who became less than themselves, or
rose to be greater than themselves by virtue of the fact that
the challenge he represented was inescapable. He is perhaps
the only black man in the world whose relationship to white
men is more terrible, more subtle, and more meaningful than
the relationship of bitter possessed to uncertain possessor.
His survival depended, and his development depends, on his
ability to turn his peculiar status in the Western world to his
own advantage and, it may be, to the very great advantage of
that world. It remains for him to fashion out of his experience
that which will give him sustenance, and a voice.

The cathedral at Chartres, I have said, says something to
the people of this village which it cannot say to me; but it is
important to understand that this cathedral says something
to me which it cannot say to them. Perhaps they are struck
by the power of the spires, the glory of the windows; but
they have known God, after all, longer than I have known
him, and in a different way, and I am terrified by the slippery
bottomless well to be found in the crypt, down which her-
etics were hurled to death, and by the obscene, inescapable

gargoyles jutting out of the stone and seeming to say that God and the devil can never be divorced. I doubt that the villagers think of the devil when they face a cathedral because they have never been identified with the devil. But I must accept the status which myth, if nothing else, gives me in the West before I can hope to change the myth.

Yet, if the American Negro has arrived at his identity by virtue of the absoluteness of his estrangement from his past, American white men still nourish the illusion that there is some means of recovering the European innocence, of returning to a state in which black men do not exist. This is one of the greatest errors Americans can make. The identity they fought so hard to protect has, by virtue of that battle, undergone a change: Americans are as unlike any other white people in the world as it is possible to be. I do not think, for example, that it is too much to suggest that the American vision of the world—which allows so little reality, generally speaking, for any of the darker forces in human life, which tends until today to paint moral issues in glaring black and white—owes a great deal to the battle waged by Americans to maintain between themselves and black men a human separation which could not be bridged. It is only now beginning to be borne in on us—very faintly, it must be admitted, very slowly, and very much against our will—that this vision of the world is dangerously inaccurate, and perfectly useless. For it protects our moral high-mindedness at the terrible expense of weakening our grasp of reality. People who shut their eyes to reality simply invite their own destruction, and anyone who insists on remaining in a state of innocence long after that innocence is dead turns himself into a monster.

The time has come to realize that the interracial drama acted out on the American continent has not only created a new black man, it has created a new white man, too. No road whatever will lead Americans back to the simplicity of this European village where white men still have the luxury of looking on me as a stranger. I am not, really, a stranger any longer for any American alive. One of the things that distinguishes Americans from other people is that no other people has ever been so deeply involved in the lives of black men, and vice versa. This fact faced, with all its implications, it can be seen that the history of the American Negro problem is not merely shameful, it is also something of an achievement. For even when the worst has been said, it must also be added that the perpetual challenge posed by this problem was always, somehow, perpetually met. It is precisely this black-white experience which may prove of indispensable value to us in the world we face today. This world is white no longer, and it will never be white again.